St George

St George

GILES MORGAN

CHARTWELL
BOOKS, INC.

This edition published in 2006 by
CHARTWELL BOOKS, INC.
A division of BOOK SALES, INC.
114 Northfield Avenue
Edison, New Jersey 08837
USA

A CIP catalogue record for this book is available from the Library of Congress.

ISBN 10: 0 7858 2232 1
EAN 13: 978 0 7858 2232 5

2 4 6 8 10 9 7 5 3 1

Typeset by Avocet Typeset, Chilton, Aylesbury, Bucks
Printed and bound in Spain

Dedicated to the memory of my grandfather
Eric J Davies

And with thanks to my wife and parents
for their help and support

Contents

Introduction

It is claimed that a vision of St George was seen during the English victory at Agincourt in 1415. Many such appearances have been ascribed to St George, from the crusades through to spectral manifestations on the battlefields of the First World War. A warrior saint, very often identified with patriotic and sometimes jingoistic concerns, he has come to be seen by many as an unequivocally English icon. His legend is evident in every aspect of society from the dedication of churches in his honour to secular representations in advertising and, particularly, in the use of his flag, the red cross of St George. And yet for all his notoriety and identification with such familiar institutions as the English village pub, he remains both an elusive and enigmatic figure.

The popularity of the story of his mythical battle with the dragon has come to obscure his origins as a real Christian martyr, who is thought to have lived around the third century AD. Persecuted by a cruel ruler for his beliefs, St George's legendary courage stems from accounts of his refusal to worship pagan gods even when faced with torture and eventual execution. Some early accounts of his life suggest that he may have been from the province of

Cappadocia in Central Turkey, others that he was Palestinian or possibly even of Nubian ancestry. The story of how an early Christian martyr from the Eastern Mediterranean came to be the patron saint of England is a fascinating if contradictory and confused one.

Some people may be surprised to find that St George is also patron saint of many other countries and is recognised on a global scale. He has been claimed by countries as diverse as Germany, Armenia, Lithuania, Portugal, Malta and Hungary. St George is the patron of Barcelona, Antioch, Genoa and many French towns. The European state of Georgia was named after him.

Closer examination of the cult of St George reveals not only his significance to a wide range of countries and societies but also some of the varying and differing roles he has fulfilled in those cultures. He has been a symbol of fertility and champion of the spring, defeating the dragon of winter, and yet he has also served as a role model of chastity. As the ultimate Christian knight, George has been depicted slaying female dragons as he fights the lustful temptations of the flesh. But his exploits have not been limited solely to Christian contexts. He has been identified with the Islamic hero Al Khidr who was said to have discovered the mythical Fountain of Youth.

As Christian martyr, St George was said to have been tortured to death (several times!), only to be resurrected by God, and his story is often linked with concepts of renewal, re-birth and revival. His legends often contain allusions to magic springs and the release of water, which has been 'held back' by the dragon and flows again when the beast is killed. The celebration of his feast day on 23 April may be connected with the coming of spring and the death of winter. Many parallels can also be drawn with pre-Christian heroes who fight terrible monsters such as Beowulf, Siegfried and Theseus, who defeats the terrible Minotaur. Close analysis of these legends shows the differing cultural values that inform them but demonstrates the seemingly universal need for a heroic figure who is lauded and revered.

St George enjoyed his greatest popularity throughout Europe in the middle ages when he was adopted by a succession of English kings and was believed to have aided Christian forces at various battles during the crusades. But St George's appeal extended to many other spheres of medieval life and he became patron of many of the important guilds of the day in cities and towns across England. His influence can be seen throughout our culture and history, from his appearance as an agricultural folk figure and staple of the mummers plays to his role as an imperialist icon in the industrial age.

St George is far from redundant today. In our multi-cultural society St George, with his own complex identity and multi-faceted history, can be seen as a strangely fitting emblem of diversity. The red cross banner of St George may, in the past, have been appropriated by right wing groups and xenophobes but, increasingly, it appears to have been embraced by a broader cross-section of society as England undergoes new political and social changes in the

21st century. The flag of St George is today most commonly seen at sporting events and in many ways has come to supersede the Union Jack as being representative of an English national identity. Football particularly has become strongly associated with the St George's flag, which is displayed on T-shirts, pennants and the painted faces of fans. Curious parallels can be drawn between George and David Beckham, a modern day icon who has both multi-cultural and national appeal. An exploration of the cult of St George reveals that it is in fact a pan-cultural phenomenon with an apparently universal popularity.

St George as Martyr

The life and identity of St George are shrouded in mystery. Very little can be said with any certainty about the real man around whom a legend has formed. And yet it is now generally accepted by most historians and writers that a real St George did exist. If these two statements seem at odds, then this is another of the many contradictory aspects of the cult of St George.

In the earliest written material about the life of St George, there is considerable variation in circumstance and detail but a basic, recognisable story can be discerned behind all the seemingly endless re-tellings. George is described as a man of high birth and rank who lived around the third or fourth century AD. He was a Christian, ordered by a pagan ruler to sacrifice to a pagan god (usually Apollo or Bacchus) who refused and was tortured and eventually beheaded for his defiance.

Almost every detail of this account changes in the surviving early Christian texts or 'hagiographies' that describe the lives of the Christian martyrs. The changes of detail are at times so bewildering that some have argued that the figure of St George never actually existed at all. However, there are also powerfully persuasive reasons for believing that St George was a real person who met his death as a Christian martyr.

Before examining the early texts in detail, it is worth outlining some of the general statements made about his cult. It is widely stated that St George was martyred at the town of Lydda in Palestine. Today this town is known as Lod and, during the Roman occupation, was referred to as Diospolis. A cult of St George centred on Lydda has existed since the early Christian period and this alone lends weight to the belief that St George existed. It was a centre of pilgrimage and worship and a Greek orthodox church dedicated in his honour can still be visited, standing in close proximity to a modern airport. Lydda lies 24 miles from Jerusalem and is located on the plain of Sharon. St George is also often linked with the town of Joppa, whose modern name is Jaffa and which stands about 12 miles from Lydda.

Another location that is consistently linked with St George is the region of Cappadocia which forms part of central Turkey. (The name Cappadocia was first used when the area was part of the Roman Empire.) However, in the centuries since the death of the saint, which is generally said to have taken place on 23 April 303 AD, the tradition of referring to St George of Cappadocia has given rise to much confusion and controversy. The confusion about St George's links with Cappadocia arises from the fact that it is known that another George of Cappadocia definitely existed. Most famously, Edward Gibbon linked the two figures in his epic *The History of the Decline and Fall of the Roman*

Empire (1776–1788). The identification of the two men is something that the humanist Gibbon seems to have taken spiteful delight in, because the historically recorded George of Cappadocia was a heretical Archbishop of Alexandria of dubious character. He is recorded as having sold 'questionable' pork to the Roman Army and was known to have been a believer in the Arian heresy. The Arians formed a religious sect that doubted that Jesus Christ had been anything other than a mortal man. This George of Cappadocia was murdered at the hands of a raging mob in 362 AD.

Gibbon enjoyed undermining some of the more fanciful aspects of Christian belief but he is now thought to be mistaken in connecting the two figures. The long tradition of St George's martyrdom at Lydda tends to contradict Gibbon's assertions. The George who was Archbishop of Alexandria has never been linked to this area. Perhaps most conclusively from a modern perspective, the discovery in the nineteenth century of two early churches dedicated to St George in Syria tends to discredit the theory that he came from Cappadocia. A church at Shakka in Syria had a Greek inscription over its doorway that stated that it was 'the house of the holy and triumphant martyrs, George and the saints who suffered martyrdom with him.'(Budge, *George of Lydda*, p.15).

The second inscription, also written in Greek, at Ezra (Azra or Adhra) describes how this previously pagan temple had been re-dedicated to St George. The translation makes for fascinating reading and states that:

1. The habitation of demons hath become a house of God.
2. A saving light hath shone in the place where darkness was enshrouded.
3. Where there were sacrifices of idols there are now a choir of angels.
4. Where God was roused to wrath He is now propitiated.
5. A certain man, a lover of Christ, the noble John, the son of Diomedes.
6. As a gift from his own money he hath offered to God a building meet to be seen.
7. Having placed therein the honourable relic(s) of the splendidly triumphant holy martyr George, who appeared to John himself.
8. Not as in a sleep (or a dream) but visibly.

(Quoted in Budge, *George of Lydda*, p.16).

The appearance of St George to his believers and supporters will rapidly become a recognisable aspect of his cult. Perhaps unsurprisingly, accurate dating of the churches has proved difficult. Some scholars have dated them to around 346 AD but others have suggested they were dedicated as late as 515 AD. As I said earlier, little can be said with certainty of the 'real' St George. However, the possibility that a known heretical Archbishop would have been made a saint and adopted with such fervent belief seems unlikely. It may be that details of his life were mistakenly grafted on to the life of St George.

The earliest written source that may relate to St George is supplied by the chronicler Eusebius of Caesarea writing in 322 AD. He tells of 'a man of the greatest distinction' who was ordered to be executed by the Emperor Diocletian at Nicomedia on 23 April 303. However, he does not record the name of the man, where he was born or even where his body was buried.

The earliest known written account of the life of St George was found in an incomplete manuscript under a pillar in the Cathedral of Qasr Ibrim in 1964. Excavations had been taking place there prior to the building of the Aswan Dam. This narrative, written in Greek, has been dated to the years between 350 and 500 AD. The manuscript describes George as being the son of a Cappadocian who lived in Nobatia, Northern Nubia, an area that forms part of the Nile valley between Khartoum and Aswan. It states that he was born during the reign of Aurelian (270–275 AD) and that he was baptised as a Christian by his mother Polychronia. This was done secretly without the knowledge of his father Gerontius who was opposed to it. George enters the Imperial Service and rises rapidly through the ranks. Later he travels to the city of Diospolis or Lydda to gain promotion. On reaching the court of Diospolis he finds that a pagan ruler has issued a decree sentencing Christians to death. George denounces the worship of Apollo at court and is arrested and gruesomely tortured. He is forced into iron-spiked shoes, his skull is crushed and he is scourged. However, the Archangel Michael heals his wounds and frees him from his imprisonment. As a result of this miracle and St George's preaching following his ordeals, a great number of people convert to

Christianity. Even the wife of the pagan ruler becomes a Christian. St George attacks the temples dedicated to Apollo and Heracles and is then beheaded by order of the furious ruler. Many who have converted are similarly punished. This version of the life of St George describes him as having lived in the same region of Nubia as other warrior saints, such as Mercurius, Theodore and Demetrius, who were all martyred as Christians by the Emperors Diocletian and Decian.

During the reign of the Emperor Diocletian, who ruled between 284 and 305 AD, Christianity had been widely accepted. It was the religion of many, even those of high status. Indeed Diocletian's wife and daughter were both Christians. But this tolerant attitude changed when a number of Christian soldiers were accused of disobeying commands and a number were killed as punishment for this around 300 AD. Events worsened when a plot emerged that appeared to involve Christians. Diocletian issued an edict that Christians were to be banned from meeting and worshipping and ordered the destruction of churches and religious texts. Every soldier was instructed to make proper sacrifice to the gods of Rome.

Diocletian ordered the Praetorian Guard to destroy the great Cathedral of Nicomedia and this was carried out on 23 February 303 AD. The emperor's edict was brutally enforced across the Roman Empire. These events may form the background to the martyrdom of St George, although some, including Sir Ernest Wallis Budge, have argued for a different date. Budge, who was the author of *George of*

Lydda, the Patron Saint of England (1930), was also keeper of Near Eastern Manuscripts at the British Museum. He was an important figure in the history of research relating to St George and believed that the generally accepted date of his martyrdom (23 April 303) was incorrect. He argued that the martyrdom had taken place 50 years before that date.

Another important early Christian text relating to the life of St George is known as the Vienna Palimpsest. (A palimpsest is a manuscript which has had its text erased and new material written onto it.) This manuscript is written in Greek and dates from the fifth century. Like other similar works from this and later centuries, it describes events in terms that veer away from realistic detail and move further towards fantasy. Yet, this version is thought to have proved very influential on later accounts of the martyrdom of St George. It purports to have as its basis another document which was written by, or perhaps more properly, authenticated by a servant of George called Pasicrates. (This was a tactic used quite frequently by writers of the lives of the saints, the hagiographers, to lend their accounts gravity and credulity.) In this version, George is again identified as being of Cappadocian extraction but is said to have lived in Palestine.

He has excelled within the Imperial Army and seeks promotion from the ruler Dadianos. Once again, the pagan ruler has attacked and banned Christianity and has ordered his subjects to give sacrifice to the gods. George is defiant, gives away his money and belongings and refuses to sacrifice. In this account, George becomes engaged in a heated argument with the emperor about his actions and is cruelly tortured. A magician called Athanasius gives him poison but he is unaffected by it.

As a result Athanasius is converted to Christianity and put to death by Dadianos. St George is killed on a wheel fitted with knives but he is restored to life by the Archangel Michael and the Lord. When St George appears before the king, his general Anatolius and his entire army convert to Christianity. They too are executed. Dadianos has molten lead poured down the throat of St George who, once again, survives through the help of God. The significance of this account is that it establishes the tradition that George suffers four deaths, is resurrected three times by the Lord and gains his martyr's crown on the fourth occasion. The saint is also described as having the power to resurrect the dead himself and also causes a number of wooden thrones to grow roots, flower and bring forth fruit. The miracles that George performs persuade the Empress Alexandra and many thousands to convert to Christianity.

The evil ruler Dadianos is often described as being a terrible tyrant or dragon and this could be one origin of the much later medieval account of St George's fight with the dragon. The 'Princess' or 'Empress' Alexandra is converted from the worship of Apollo to Christianity by St George and so is 'saved' by him. Interestingly, there is a tradition within the imagery of Greek Orthodox icons that portrays St George on horseback trampling down a man with a sword and shield rather than the mythical dragon.

Sir Ernest Wallis Budge argued that the Babylonian Epic

of Gilgamesh influenced the story of the martyrdom of St George. The hero Gilgamesh was two-thirds god and one-third mortal man. Budge suggested that early followers of the cult of the saint may have identified him with the Babylonian hero, 'If St George were three parts God and one part man, the four killings would be understandable'. (Budge, *George of Lydda*, p.43).

Ironically, the increasingly fantastical nature of the stories of George's martyrdom led to the first definite reference to the saint that we have. In 494 AD Pope Gelasius produced the first Index or list of works that were believed to be apocryphal. The 'Passio Giorgi' is amongst them. Gelasius condemned certain lives or 'Acta' as being absurd because of their increased tendency towards fiction and sensationalism. However, he concluded, significantly, that George was to be grouped with saints 'whose names are justly reverenced among men, but whose actions are known only to God'. As well as a dismissal of the extravagant claims made for him, this is an acknowledgement that a 'real' St George did exist. However, the efforts of Gelasius and his council to control and limit the accounts of the life of St George that were circulating were largely ignored and subsequent martyrologies proved to be just as fantastical. George's conflict with a human foe metamorphosed over time into a fully-fledged fantasy about battles with dragons.

Another possible influence on the development of the cult of St George is thought to have been the Roman Emperor Constantine the Great who was born on 27

February 272 AD and died on 22 May 337 AD. Constantine is often referred to as the first Christian Emperor. As a young man Constantine served at the court of Diocletian in Nicomedia. His father, Constantius, later became emperor and, when Constantius was in Britain, campaigning against the Scots and Picts of Caledonia, he became ill and subsequently died. The day Constantius died, 25 July 306 AD, was the day Constantine was proclaimed 'Augustus', or Emperor, at York in Britain by his loyal troops. Constantine became Western Emperor, since the Empire was divided at this time into two halves, Eastern and Western. During his career Constantine re-founded Byzantium, which came to be known as 'Constantinopolis' ('Constantine's city'), on the site of modern day Istanbul. Constantine held the Council of Nicea in 325 AD, an event that legalised Christianity throughout the Empire for the first time in history. The Council of Nicea, together with the earlier Edict of Milan, issued in 313 AD, were instrumental in paving the way for the growth of Christianity.

Constantine the Great is reported to have built a church at Lydda in honour of St George. Sir Ernest Wallis Budge, amongst others, have suggested that the church contained a bas-relief of Constantine which depicted him standing on top of a dragon or serpent and holding the banner of the Cross in his right hand. It is thought that early followers of St George's cult, either intentionally or accidentally, may have identified this sculptural image with the saint and the result was a merging of the imagery of the two figures.

It is also worth noting that a number of Roman coins depict human figures standing over the body of a serpent. Valentinian III is shown on a gold 'solidus' in just such a pose with his right foot on top of a serpent with a human head. In his right hand he is holding a cross and, in his left, he is holding an orb decorated with an angel of victory. A bronze coin struck during the reign of Constantine shows the Emperor transfixing a serpent with the 'labarum', an early Christian motif.

The Edict of Milan in 313 AD, issued by Constantine, had granted religious tolerance and freedom but Licinius, who was the Emperor of the Eastern Roman Empire, broke the agreement in 320 AD. He began to persecute Christians, a policy that finally resulted in the civil war of 324 AD. It became a war of religions as Constantine's army fought under the banner of the labarum against the pagan armies of Licinius. Constantine and his troops emerged as the victors and this is often viewed as marking the end of the pagan Empire and the beginning of a new Christian era. However, many at the court of Constantine retained pagan beliefs and the Emperor himself, earlier in his career, used the Roman gods Mars and Apollo in his official representations.

Other traditions, usually regarded with some scepticism, are said to link Constantine and St George with Britain. It is sometimes said, for example, that Constantine formed an order called the Constantinian Angelic Knights of St George in 312 AD and Geoffrey of Monmouth, in his twelfth century *History of the Kings of Britain*, wrote that the mother of Constantine, Helena, was actually the daughter of 'Old King Cole' who founded Colchester and had been ruler of the Britons. Geoffrey's claims are largely spurious – inventions designed to create a noble lineage for the British kings. He also claimed that Constantine was made 'King of the Britons' at York rather than Roman Emperor.

During the medieval period stories developed that St George had travelled to England as a tribune in the Roman army on the orders of Diocletian. He is said to have been a friend of Helena, the Empress who, it was claimed, discovered the 'True Cross' upon which Christ was crucified. This friendship, according to tradition, led her to build a church to St George in Jerusalem adjoining or near to the Church of the Holy Sepulchre. This story reflects the development of the cult of St George in England and his gradual identification with the country of which he would later become patron saint. Other traditions claim that St George visited the tomb of Joseph of Arimathea, who was his relative, at Glastonbury. St George is also said to have travelled to the Roman garrison town of Caerleon-on-Usk in south Wales. The British chronicler Gildas describes Caerleon as having been a centre of Christianity in the early fourth century. Other traditions claim that St George and Constantine had served together under Diocletian and had been based at York.

The reputation of St George, as the epitome of bravery and the champion of Christ and the poor and defenceless, spread widely in the centuries following the believed date of his martyrdom. The sixth century historian Procopius records that the Emperor Justinian built a church in his honour in Armenia and, in France, Clovis (466–511 AD), the founder of the Merovingian dynasty, built a monastery in the saint's honour at Baralle. Pope Zacharias (741–752 AD) found the head of St George the martyr in a reliquary in the Lateran Palace. (The reliquary was identified by a Greek inscription that described its contents. It was to be one amongst many such reliquaries containing innumerable heads and bones of the martyr that would be discovered. Some of them may even have been authentic.) Its appearance at least attests to the veneration of the saint at this time. The English historian the Venerable Bede (673–735), records St George in his martyrology. He describes the saint as having been martyred on 23 April by the ruler Dacian (or Datian) who is called a 'Persian king'. Bede also includes a story told by Adamnan, who was Abbot of Iona in 679 AD. From a bishop called Arculf, who had been to Lydda and visited the shrine of St George, the abbot had heard of a miracle. Arculf related that a man had promised to hand over his horse to St George in exchange for the saint's protection as he travelled from Diospolis. However, the man reneged on his promise and St George made the horse wild and unmanageable, so forcing the man to keep his vow. Arculf would also have seen the statue of Constantine in the church of St George.

The Anglo-Saxon writer Aelfric produced an account of the life of St George around the year 1000 AD. He describes the saint as being a 'rich eorldorman, under the fierce Datianus, in the shire of Cappadocia'. A monastery dedicated to St George was founded at Thetford whilst Canute was king (1017–1035). It is also known that a church of St George was in existence during the Anglo-Saxon period in Southwark in South London. Budge reported that a church of St George had been built at Windsor before the first crusade and that the Collegiate Church at Oxford had been dedicated to St George after the Norman invasion in 1074.

It is worth noting that not all early accounts of the life of St George refer to him as a soldier. The earliest known image of the saint is a Byzantine icon of the sixth century that shows him on the right hand side of the Virgin who is accompanied on her left by St Theodore. Although both are known as soldier saints Samantha Riches has noted that St George 'is not obviously presented as a military figure, although it has been argued that armour is discernible beneath their robes'. (Samantha Riches, *St George, Hero, Martyr and Myth*, p.12).

St George may or may not have been a military figure but the themes of bravery and courage linked to his stories are undeniable. In Greek, George is referred to as the 'megalomartyr' meaning the great martyr and, in the Greek and Russian Orthodox churches, he is known as the 'victory bearer' and the 'trophy bearer'. An Irish martyrology of the ninth century also records his association with the theme of triumph. In it, a writer called Oengus describes him as 'a sun of victories'. St George's reputation for courage, which stemmed from the accounts of his refusal to desert his faith, would be the defining feature of the breath-taking growth of the cult that surrounded him. His powers as intercessor, defender of the faith and, as we shall see in later chapters, his abilities as a healer would win him many followers in countries as diverse as Egypt, Ethiopia, Spain, Hungary, Italy, Germany, Portugal, Syria and, of course, England.

Early Christian Saints

In exploring the development of the cult of St George, it is important to look at the earliest Christian practices of the veneration of saints. A saint is an individual who has either died as a martyr defending his or her faith and beliefs or someone who has lived a life of great holiness and piety. Often the lives of the saints are linked to miracles and the performance of great acts of courage or healing. Christians suffered great persecution in the first few centuries following the death of Christ and the earliest of all saints are generally martyrs who gave their lives for their religious beliefs. At first the cult of a saint was established unofficially through his or her popularity within the Christian community but, by the twelfth and thirteenth centuries, the status of saint could only be granted by the papacy. The Holy See judged the case for canonisation on the basis of the merits and values of the life of the individual and also by examining claims of miracles that they were said to have performed. (Much the same procedure is followed in the Roman Catholic church today.)

Early Christian funerals involved the burial of the dead rather than cremation. They were group events overseen by the leaders of the community where the Eucharist would be celebrated. Significantly the anniversary of the day of the individual's death, often through violent martyrdom, was observed rather than the birth date. Importantly, martyrs were venerated as mortal men and women who had joined God after their deaths and so achieved eternal life. However, over time, the belief grew that the saints had important powers of intercession and could act as a link between God and living Christians. In this sense, the status of the saints was altered as the devout began to pray to them for comfort and aid. The practice of preserving the bones of the saint as holy relics grew and, increasingly, they were interred under the altars of churches. The earliest account of the martyrdom of a saint that is believed to be authentic is that of Polycarp who was executed for his beliefs in 155 AD. He was a follower of John the disciple and, following his death at the hands of a pagan official, his body was burnt but importantly his remains were collected by other Christians and venerated.

In England, St Alban ranks amongst the earliest of Christian martyrs. He is thought to have been martyred around the end of the third century AD. The early chroniclers, Bede and Gildas, both state that this happened during the reign of the Roman Emperor Diocletian, about 300 AD. Alban is said to have sheltered a fugitive Christian priest and then been converted and baptised by him. In order to help the priest escape, Alban, who was a Roman citizen of the town of Verulamium in England, impersonated him by dressing in his clothes. Alban was arrested and, after refusing to sacrifice to the Roman gods, was beheaded in the amphitheatre outside the modern cathedral city of St Albans in Hertfordshire, which today bears his name. Some claim that the saint asked for water before his execution and was denied it, only for a spring to appear magically. It is also said that, after he had been beheaded, the eyes of his executioner popped out of his head! At the beginning of the eleventh century a certain Abbot Ealdred of St Albans wrote that, in the course of rebuilding his abbey with stones from the ruins of Verulamium, he had 'flattened as far as he was able the den of the Dragon of Wormenhert, so dispelling for ever traces of the serpent's lair'. (Ralph Whitlock, *Here Be Dragons*, p.106). The dragon is also mentioned in later medieval histories of the monastery. It is possible that this curious historical fragment may record an oral tradition or legend, which derives from the martyrdom of St Alban under the draconian rule of a repressive Roman emperor. In modern representations of the saint he is often depicted as a soldier.

St Edward the Confessor is of particular relevance to the story of St George in that he preceded him as the patron saint of England. Before the adoption of George during the middle ages, this was a role Edward shared with St Edmund. Edward was the son of Ethelred the Unready and ruled England from 1042 to 1066. Although Edward was the son of an Anglo-Saxon king his mother, Emma, was of Norman descent. During his reign Edward managed to maintain peace for more than twenty years and was famed for his kindness to his subjects. He was also the founder of

Westminster Abbey where his relics are still held today. His mixed parentage made him a popular figure with both the Anglo-Saxons and the invading Normans and it was claimed in 1102 that his body had remained incorrupt. He was canonised in 1161 at the request of Henry II who was a blood relative of Edward's.

Edmund was an English king of Saxon descent who lived from 841 to 869 AD and practised the Christian faith. He is thought to have become the king of the East Angles prior to 865 AD and fought an invading Viking force in 869–870 AD. His army was defeated and Edmund was taken prisoner. He is reputed to have refused to give into Viking demands to serve as a puppet king and would not deny his faith in Christianity. For this he was tortured and killed. Some accounts claim he was scourged with hot irons or more famously that he was shot to death with arrows before being beheaded. Other grisly legends describe him meeting his death through the Viking practice of the 'spread-eagle' or 'blood-eagle' where the victim's chest was cut open and his lungs pulled out as a sacrifice to pagan gods. Another legend states that, following his decapitation in a forest, his head was protected by a wolf. Followers of Edmund found the head later and re-joined it to his body. The miraculously incorrupt corpse was taken to Bury St Edmunds (known formerly as Bedricsworth) where it was interred and a shrine to the king created. His popularity stemmed from his commitment to Christianity and his defiant spirit of English independence in the face of aggressive incomers.

The importance of the two kings as protectors of England is illustrated by a surviving medieval panel painting generally referred to as the 'Wilton Diptych' or to give its full title, 'Richard II presented to the Virgin and Child by his Patron John the Baptist and Saints Edward and Edmund'. Created in the late 1390s, it offers a fascinating insight into the medieval concept of divine protection and favour and is full of symbolic meaning. The diptych is formed of two panels joined together, that open and close much like a book, and it is thought it was intended for the private use of Richard II as an icon of devotion. On the left panel, Richard II is kneeling before the saints and looking across to the right panel at the Virgin Mary and Jesus who is pictured as a child. St Edward is holding a ring that he was reputed to have given to St John the Evangelist. To the far left St Edmund holds an arrow, the symbol of his martyrdom. On the right hand panel, the Christ child appears to be blessing Richard II and is surrounded by a host of angels. On the left of this panel is a standard that bears the Red Cross flag on a white background. It is thought that this flag may represent either St George or the resurrection of Christ, or both.

There is an interesting pictorial example of Christ himself, emerging from his tomb and holding the Red Cross flag, in a panel of the Santa Croce Altarpiece from Florence in Italy, painted in about 1324–1325, that illustrates the flag's more general meaning as the symbol of the martyr and of the resurrection. At the top of the standard in the Wilton Diptych is set an orb and cleaning and restoration of the painting in 1992 revealed a previously unrecognised feature on the panel. On closer inspection of the orb the restorers found that it contained a minute picture of a castle on a green island surrounded by a silvery sea with a small boat floating on the waves. It is thought that the island probably represents England and that Richard II is symbolically placing it under the protection of the Virgin and Child and St George. Although this cannot be taken as a complete certainty, it is worth noting that, in Christian iconography and church dedications, St George is often linked to the Virgin Mary, and Richard II was amongst the English kings who promoted his importance as patron of England. This is further supported by descriptions of a lost altarpiece of a similar date that is reputed to have shown Richard II alongside St George and a number of other saints.

The patron saint of Ireland is, of course, St Patrick, another Christian figure around whom a great deal of myth and legend has grown up. He is credited with having thrown the snakes out of Ireland and, in some accounts, with having single-handedly converted the entire country to the Christian faith. He lived and preached during the fifth century and was born in Britain 'somewhere in the west between the mouth of the Severn and the Clyde, called Bannavem Taburniae'. (David Farmer, *Oxford Dictionary of Saints*, p389). As a teenager Patrick was captured by an Irish raiding party and forced to become a slave in Ireland. He spent six years in slavery and either managed eventually to escape or, possibly, was set free. In a prophetic dream he was shown that he would return to Britain and so he made his way back to his family where he trained as a priest. St Patrick was not the first Christian missionary to be sent by the church to Ireland. St Palladius was a bishop who was appointed by Pope Celestine I in 431 AD to accomplish the task of converting the heathen Irish. However, his mission proved short-lived. Landing in Wicklow, he founded three churches there but left not long after and sailed to Scotland where he died. St Palladius is now linked to Aberdeen where a cult sprang up around him following his death. It is thought Palladius's mission to Ireland failed either due to hostility to Christianity or because the saint himself had little enthusiasm for the role. Although Christianity had reached Ireland at this time, the church had not established strong, settled roots there. Patrick began his mission in 435 AD, basing himself in County Armagh in Northern Ireland. He devoted himself to the suppression and destruction of paganism and other heathen acts such as the worship of the sun. The symbolic story of him banishing the snakes from Ireland probably derives from his battle to defeat the old religion and to establish the Christian church in the island. Patrick's mission was a dangerous one and he wrote that he often expected either to be murdered or enslaved but was prepared to embrace martyrdom in the service of Christ.

Scotland's adoption of St Andrew as its patron saint is based on a far more tenuous connection. Andrew was one of the apostles of Christ who had worked as a fisherman and had been a follower of John the Baptist. Very little is known about his life, although he is said to have preached in Greece and is linked to Epirus and Scythia. He is supposed to have been crucified at Patras in Achaia for his beliefs. He survived for two days on the cross where he continued to preach to an assembled crowd. In many early images of his martyrdom St Andrew is shown being crucified on a normal cross but, in later examples, he is depicted upon an x-shaped cross, also known as the 'saltire' cross. A popular legend states that his relics were taken to Scotland and a church built in his honour in Fife. Some accounts have them carried there by angels. The shrine became the town of St Andrew's and it became an important centre for Christianity. Because of this legend, Andrew, neither a native Scot nor even a visitor to the country in his lifetime, became its patron saint. Since it was believed he had died on a saltire cross the Scottish flag was devised as an x-shaped white cross on a blue background, a design which is also integrated into the Union Jack.

St Michael ranks alongside St George as the most famous dragon-slayer in Christian iconography. In the book of Revelation, Michael and his angels are described as throwing the devil, in the form of a dragon, out of heaven and down to the surface of the earth. In the New Testament Letter of Jude he is said to have contended with the devil for the body of Moses, crying out, 'the Lord rebuke you!' (Jude 9). The name Michael means 'Who is like unto God'. He is credited with being the guardian angel of Israel in the Old Testament book of Daniel and is referred to as, 'the great prince', (Daniel 12: 1) and 'one of the chief princes', (Daniel 10: 13). Michael's powers were said to be so great that, in a second century Christian text called *The Testament of Abraham*, he is even able to rescue souls from hell. He is often depicted in paintings, carvings and sculptures, dressed in armour and armed with a sword or lance, standing on top of, or over, a dragon. In the painting 'Saint Michael' by the Italian artist Piero della Francesca, dating from about 1415, he is shown holding the decapitated head of a serpent and standing upon the creature's body. The treatment of the scene here is semi-realistic, although he is holding the snake's head by one of its horns. Interestingly, St Michael is portrayed wearing the uniform and armour of a Roman soldier from the classical period rather than being depicted in medieval armour. The snake, of course, represents the devil, whom Michael has conquered.

The Spanish artist Bartolome Bermejo created a much more macabre and fantastical image of the devil in his painting 'Saint Michael triumphant over the devil with the Donor Antonio Juan' of 1468. The devil is shown as a strange, grotesque hybrid of bat and reptile, with staring red eyes and a curling tail that is wrapped around the saint's right leg. Michael is depicted in medieval armour, holding aloft his sword whilst the 'Donor Antonio Juan' kneels in prayer nearby. Antonio Juan was the Lord of the Spanish town of Tous near Valencia and the image is taken from the central panel of the altarpiece in the parish church.

St Michael is sometimes confused with St George because he is often pictured with a dragon or snake but the two can be differentiated in iconography by the fact that Michael, as an archangel, usually has wings. In some medieval images St Michael is shown weighing human souls on a set of scales. He often appears as a stern, forbidding figure, ready to do battle for God or to judge the lives of mankind. He is known as a powerful intercessor whose help can be called upon by those in need. At the monastery dedicated to St Michael on the Greek Island of Symi, local tradition states that, if you ask for help from the archangel, you must also give him a gift or offering in return. Michael is the patron saint of the island and of seafarers, and the votive offerings of those seeking his aid often take the form of models of ships made from gold and silver.

In Greece, the archangel Michael has, like St George, been very popular, perhaps partly because of his martial prowess and reputation for protection and because of the long history of conflict between the Greeks and the Turkish. The island of Lesvos is home to a famous 'black' icon of Michael that is said to have been created from mud and the blood of monks who were killed in a raid by the Ottomans. Michael is a part of Islamic, as well as Judaic and Christian, tradition, being one of the archangels referred to in the Koran, where he is called 'Mika'il'.

St Michael's high position as captain of the heavenly host is often reflected in the geographical choice of sites that are dedicated to him. The summit of Glastonbury Tor has a tower dedicated to him and the island peaks of St Michael's Mount in Cornwall and Mont Saint Michel off the coast of Normandy are both named in his honour. St Michael's Mount was said to be the site of an eighth century apparition of the archangel and a similar claim has been made for

Mont St Michel. His cult is particularly strong in Cornwall and the town of Helston has a number of legends that concern St Michael's victory over the devil. A large boulder built into the wall of a local hotel is said to have been thrown by the devil at the saint and is known as the Hell's Stone because it blocked the entrance to Hell. During the battle at Helston, the devil is said to have taken the form of a dragon, which St Michael defeated.

The early Irish Christian monastery on the inhospitable rocky Atlantic island of Great Skellig is dedicated to him and is often called 'Skellig Michael'. Other examples include St Michael's church on Highgate Hill in London and the Monastery of St Michael on the Greek island of Thasos, which is situated on a rocky coastal crag. The Monastery of St Michael is situated in view of Mount Athos, one of the most sacred Christian sites in Greece. On the Ionian island of Corfu the twelfth century Byzantine fortress of Angelokastro is thought to take its name from the archangels Michael and Gabriel. (In Greek 'angelo' means angel and 'kastro' a castle.) The fortress is situated on a rocky pinnacle 300 metres above the sea. A tiny church dedicated to the archangels is located at the top of the upper keep.

The cult of St Michael spread from the East across Europe to the West in the early Christian period and, like that of George, reached its peak during the medieval period. His feast day is 29 September and this 'commemorates the dedication of his basilica on the Salarian way near Rome'. (David Farmer, *Oxford Dictionary of Saints*, p.348)

In 1969 the Roman Catholic Church combined his feast day with that of the archangels Gabriel and Raphael.

The lives of many of the saints feature much invention and imaginative content. However, St Margaret, who is also supposed to have killed a dragon, probably never existed at all. The story of Margaret of Antioch, as she is often known, is almost certainly a work of religious fiction and, as early as 494 AD, Pope Gelasius declared her life and legend apocryphal. However, the nature of her legend and her popularity in England and Europe make her worthy of consideration for the insights her story offers into the beliefs and traditions of medieval Christianity.

St Margaret was said to have lived in the city of Antioch and was the 'daughter of Theodosius, patriarch of the pagans'. (Jacobus de Voragine, *The Golden Legend* p.162). She was baptised as a child, an event that angered and embittered her father. When she was fifteen, a local prefect called Olybrius came upon her by chance while she was tending some sheep. Olybrius was smitten by her great beauty and declared he would marry her if she was free born or take her for his harem if she was a slave. He remarked that her name, which comes from the Latin 'margarita', meaning pearl, was fitting and appropriate because of her beauty. However, upon discovering her commitment to the Christian faith and her refusal to worship pagan gods, Olybrius had Margaret thrown in jail. The next day, he again demanded that she abandon Christ and worship his gods and, once again, she refused. Margaret was then cruelly tortured and, as in so many lives of the saints, her torture is described in often salacious and sensationalist detail. According to Jacobus de Voragine, 'her flesh was raked with iron combs until the bones were laid bare and the blood gushed from her body as if from the purest spring' (*The Golden Legend*, p.162).

However, St Margaret withstood the torture with her faith intact and the prefect, who was sickened by the sight of her injuries, ordered that she be taken off the rack. Back in her cell she suddenly witnessed a magical, radiant light and Margaret prayed to the Lord to reveal the enemy that was fighting against her. A terrible dragon appeared and made to devour her but, by making the sign of the cross, Margaret made the monster vanish. (A popular variation of the story that often appears in medieval paintings has St Margaret actually swallowed whole by the dragon. Inside the belly of the beast Margaret arms herself with a cross and the dragon bursts asunder and she emerges unharmed.) After appearing as a dragon the devil changed his shape to that of a man and tried to persuade Margaret to abandon Christ. She refused and, seizing him, hurls him to the ground, famously putting her foot on his neck and commanding him to lie under 'the foot of a woman'. Because her refusal to give in was leading to many thousands converting to Christianity, the prefect had Margaret beheaded but not before she prayed to God that any woman who is in childbirth and invokes her name should be protected and have a healthy child. All this was alleged to have happened during the reign of Diocletian. St Margaret also promised that she would protect those who invoked her name on their deathbeds and safeguard their passage to heaven and that she would assist those who dedicated churches or prayers to her. Her famed abilities as a powerful protector and intercessor made her a popular saint during the Middle Ages. Joan of Arc claimed that St Margaret was one of the voices that spoke to her in her visions.

St George is one of a number of early Christian warrior-saints to become popular during the middle ages. The lives of such figures share remarkable similarities and it is gener-ally accepted that the hagiographies of the saints often used references to, and borrowings from, earlier texts when they were compiled. St Demetrius was said to have been a Roman soldier who embraced Christianity and was mar-tyred for it during the reign of Maximian in the early fourth century. He is reputed to have inspired others to give their lives in defence of their faith. Demetrius was a popular saint in the east (he was martyred at Mitrovica in Serbia) and he is the patron saint of Macedonia, Bulgaria and Belgrade. One story relates that St Demetrius helped pro-tect Thessalonika from Slav soldiers in 586 AD by appear-ing on a white horse in shining armour and leading the defenders to victory even though they were outnumbered. At a shrine in Thessalonika, holy oil was reputed to flow from the bones of the saint. Mount Athos also holds relics of this heroic martyr who has over 200 churches dedicated in his honour in the Balkans. His popularity spread to the West during the crusades.

St Theodore is another soldier saint about whom very little is known save that he was a soldier who was martyred for his Christian faith during the fourth century. In another echo of the life of Saint George, he is said to have refused to worship pagan gods and destroyed a heathen temple by setting fire to it. As a result of his sacrilegious actions he was tortured cruelly and died of his wounds.

Saint George and the Dragon

For many people, the martyrdom of St George has come to be largely overshadowed, if not completely obscured, by his legendary conflict with a fearsome dragon. His fabled encounter with this terrifying beast is a later addition to the cult of St George and an episode in the life of the saint that was popularised particularly by the Dominican Prior Jacobus de Voragine. His book *Legenda Aurea* or *The Golden Legend*, completed in about 1266, was a collection of the lives of the saints and other related material. It was a hugely popular work during the later middle ages and many copies were made of it in manuscript form before the advent of printing. *The Golden Legend* describes the glorious death of St George as a Christian martyr but begins with his battle with the dragon.

In order to examine the themes and ideas within the legend, it is important to summarise the content of Jacobus de Voragine's version of the tale. George is said to be a tribune in the Roman army from the region of Cappadocia who comes one day to the city of Silena in Libya. The city is being terrorised by a monstrous dragon that lives in a huge lake close by. Although the citizens have attempted to fight the dragon they cannot overcome it and the creature regularly approaches the city walls and suffocates the people with its poisonous breath. They have taken to placating the dragon by feeding it two sheep a day. If they do not feed the dragon it rushes at the walls and blasts the city's inhabitants with its foul breath. As their flocks become depleted the people take to feeding the dragon just one sheep and one person. Lots are drawn to select the unfortunate individual.

Eventually all the young people of the city have been consumed by the dragon apart from the king's daughter and a crowd gathers to take her to be fed to the monster. The king, who has ordered that the young people of the city should be sacrificed in this way to allay the fury of the dragon, bewails the fate of his daughter and pleads that she should be spared. The people are angered that he should allow their children to die but attempt to save his own. He asks that they allow him to have a reprieve of one week in which to mourn his daughter and they agree to this. The king is overcome with grief that he will never see his daughter's wedding day but, at the end of the week of grace, the people demand that he hand her over to be given to the dragon. She is dressed in great finery and then leaves the city and approaches the lake where the dragon lives.

St George, who is travelling past the scene, sees the princess weeping and stops to ask her why she is crying. She urges him to flee and warns him he will be killed with her but St George refuses to leave and asks her why she is waiting near the lake and why the people of the city are watching. The princess explains what is happening and St George promises to help her. As they are talking the dragon emerges from the lake and George, making the sign of the cross, mounts his horse and rides out to challenge the creature as it rushes to attack him. St George deals a terrible blow to the dragon with his lance and it is hurled, wounded, to the ground. The saint calls out to the princess not to be afraid and to throw her girdle around the neck of the injured dragon, which she does. She then leads the defeated dragon into the city. At first, this causes panic amongst the inhabitants. As the people are fleeing Saint George calls out to them, 'Do not be afraid... The Lord has sent me to free you from the tyranny of the dragon. Only believe in Christ and be baptised, every one of you, and I will slay your dragon!' (Jacobus de Voragine, *The Golden Legend*, p.117).

The king and the people agree to be baptised and St George kills the dragon with his sword and gives orders for it to be carried outside the city walls. The dragon is so huge that it takes four pairs of oxen to drag its body to a plain beyond the city. Equally vast are the numbers who turn to Christ. 'That day twenty thousand were baptised, not counting women and children. The king built a large and splendid church there in honour of Blessed Mary and St George, and from its altar there still issues a natural spring whose waters cure all illnesses.' (Jacobus de Voragine, *The Golden Legend*, p.117). St George refuses to be given money for his bravery and orders his reward to be given to the poor people of the city. Before riding away St George leaves the king four rules to live by: to cherish the church of the Lord, to attend mass always, to honour the priests and to care for the poor.

This is the story Voragine tells but it must be remembered that there are many different accounts of the life of St George, from many periods in history, and that there is considerable variation in the details of them. Voragine was not the originator of this story. His work was a collection of existing stories and traditions and the concept of George defeating a dragon was already an established one. However, it is extremely difficult to establish exactly when it entered the cycle of the life of St George. Early visual representations of St George include Macedonian and Tunisian icons of the sixth and seventh centuries which depict the saint battling with a serpent. Interestingly, the saint is portrayed on horseback, spearing human enemies in an attitude that is very similar to that of his fight with the dragon, on a tympanum (the area above a door lintel and the arch that enclose it) at St George's Church at Fordington, Dorset. This tympanum dates from 1100 and is amongst the oldest recorded images of St George in England. A twelfth century carving of St George on a charger, trampling and spearing the dragon, can be found above the doorway of Brinsop church in Herefordshire. Both these images were created during the Crusades and, in all probability, relate to Christian battles in the Holy Land and reflect St George's popularity during this period. Images of dragons are relatively common in medieval churches, often symbolising earlier pagan religions and beliefs. Examples include an eleventh century tympanum which depicts an elaborate, spiralling, coiled dragon at Uppington church in Shropshire and carvings of dragons in Much Wenlock church in the same county.

Local legend claims that Brinsop is the site where St George killed the dragon. As well as the carving of this mythical event, the church, which is dedicated to the saint, has a 'dragon's well' in its grounds. (There appears to be an extremely ancient link between dragons and water in the mythologies of many cultures around the world.) Dragon Hill near the White Horse of Uffington hill figure in Wiltshire is also said to be the place where George fought the dragon. The carving of the white horse has been achieved by stripping away the vegetation and topsoil to reveal the underlying chalk. The crown of Dragon Hill is similarly bare and it is claimed that its barren appearance is due to George spilling the blood of the dragon here. It has even been argued that the White Horse hill figure is, in fact, a representation of a dragon. Other local traditions state that the dragon lies buried under the hill.

At the village church of Avebury in Wiltshire there is a carving on the font of a bishop striking or impaling a dragon with his crozier. Interestingly, the dragon appears to be aiming a bite at the bishop's foot. This worn twelfth century image could be interpreted as symbolising the victory of the Christian church over the pagan religions of the past. As the author Janet Hoult has observed, 'It is a significant find in a place of such old-religion power as Avebury, so close to the huge stone circle there, and may show the battle the Christian priests had with the old religion.' (Janet Hoult, *Dragons: Their History & Symbolism*, p.43).

The eighteenth century antiquarian William Stukeley believed that the immense Neolithic stone circle at Avebury with its attendant stone rows, the West Kennet avenue and the recently excavated Beckhampton avenue, were intended to represent a huge, coiled snake. He suggested that the nearby circle known as the Sanctuary formed the snake's head and the West Kennet avenue the neck. The creature's coiled body was symbolised by the giant Avebury ring and the tail was formed by the Beckhampton avenue of standing stones.

Dragons are apparently universal symbols that can be found in a multitude of cultures and which can be traced to the earliest belief systems and their associated stories. The word 'dragon' is derived from the Greek word for serpent, 'drakon'. In Latin this became 'draco', a large snake or dragon. Janet Hoult has also put forward the argument that the word dragon derives, 'from the verb "derkein", which means to see clearly. Dragons were credited with clear sight, wisdom and the ability to foretell the future.' (Janet Hoult, *Dragons: Their History and Symbolism*, p.6)

In an ancient Babylonian creation myth, the Great Goddess Tiamat fights the male hero-God Marduk and is killed. Tiamat is usually depicted as a great sea serpent or dragon and is closely linked to water. Her image is recorded on Babylonian cylinder seals as a monstrous crawling dragon which is being pursued by Marduk, who wields thunderbolts as weapons like the Greek god Zeus.

However, in this dragon-slaying myth, the god Marduk uses the body of Tiamat to create and bring order to the world. He splits the body of Tiamat in two, creating the sky with one half and controlling the waters with the other. Similarly, Hindu myth tells of a great conflict between a male god Indra and the dragon Vrtra. Indra's victory over Vrtra releases the waters that the dragon has been restraining and holding back with its body. In many ways, these tales are not, like the legend of St George, simply descriptions of the battle between good and evil. As Jacqueline Simpson has commented, 'the issues involved are not ethical, but cosmic; these myths are concerned with the creative process that shaped the universe and restored order after a threat of chaos...' (Jacqueline Simpson, *British Dragons*, p.20). Such ancient myths perceive creation and destruction as part of natural and interlinked patterns rather than as the dualistic struggle of Christian thought which polarises such forces into pure evil or ultimate good. The dragons of the Babylonian and Hindu creation myths are complex and awesome elemental nature deities whose lives and deaths form the basis of our world.

In Egyptian culture an example of a dragon linked to the great cycles of nature is provided by the god Apep who takes the form of a great serpent or crocodile. Each day Apep chases the sun across the sky in order to consume it and to prevent it from rising in the East in the morning. Each day he fails but tries again. Apep is said to be the serpent form of the god Set who fights to keep the sun trapped in the Underworld. Set is the brother of Osiris, a fertility god and, together, they form aspects of a continual cycle of life and death. Osiris is killed by Set but rises again in the form of his own son, the hawk-headed god Horus, and defeats Set. These Egyptian deities represent eternal cycles of life and death, birth and resurrection, in the lives of people, animals and crops. Like so many ancient legends they reflect the turning of the agricultural wheel of the seasons and its patterns of decay and renewal.

In the Christian creation story of Genesis it is, of course, a serpent that tempts Eve to eat the apple, the forbidden fruit of the tree of knowledge, which thus precipitates the fall of man and the expulsion of Adam and Eve from the Garden of Eden. The serpent is sometimes depicted in medieval paintings and illustrations with the head and torso of a woman.

The great biblical sea monster Leviathan, who appears in the Old Testament, is likely to have shaped and influenced the way in which the dragon that St George fought was imagined. Interesting parallels can also be drawn between the tale of Bel and the Dragon that formed part of the Book of Daniel and the legend of St George as described by Jacobus de Voragine and others. The story of Bel and the Dragon is not recognised by Protestants and became part of the Apocrypha but it is accepted by the Roman Catholic Church. It tells of how Daniel destroys the idol Bel and his temple, using his wit and intelligence, and illustrates the Christian belief in the futility of 'worshipping false Gods'. Daniel defeats a Babylonian dragon deity by 'making cakes of pitch, fat and hair. The dragon ate them and burst open.'

(Daniel 14:23–30). In the earliest accounts of George the martyr, the saint is said to refuse to sacrifice to pagan Gods and prays for the destruction of the temple by the Lord. His wish is granted and it is destroyed by fire from heaven. Daniel survives his ordeal in the lion's den (where he has been placed as punishment for offending the Babylonians) with the help of God. Similarly, St George survives many tortures with the help of God before choosing his final martyrdom. Both tales offer parables of the defeat of paganism. The tale of Bel and the Dragon is Greek in origin and has similar qualities to ancient Greek myths in which a wily hero, such as Odysseus or Jason, defeats his opponents through cunning and ingenuity.

The national flag of Wales features a red dragon, a symbol that seems entirely appropriate for a culture where these mythical beasts seem almost commonplace. For many different cultures dragons symbolise energy and virility and the author Michael Dames has written that 'the Welsh emblem, a red dragon... stood for individual and national libido'. (Michael Dames, *Merlin and Wales: A Magician's Landscape*, p.14.)

Perhaps the most famous legend in Welsh culture to feature dragons relates to the childhood of the wizard Merlin, advisor and seer to King Arthur. Around the fifth century AD, at a time when the Britons of the post-Roman period were being driven into Wales by the Angles and the Saxons, their leader King Vortigern fled to Snowdonia to establish a new base. Many early British chroniclers, such as Nennius and Geoffrey of Monmouth, describe how

Vortigern made deals and arrangements with these incomers who acted as mercenaries for him, but ultimately
reneged on them to seize land and power for themselves.
Vortigern's new city was to be built at Dinas Emrys on a
hill and he ordered that a tower be built there. However,
every attempt at collecting the materials to build the tower
at the site failed because they disappeared each night.
Vortigern's wizards advised him to find a child without a
father and to sacrifice him and sprinkle his blood on the
foundations. This, they said, was the only way to ensure
that the tower was built. Searching for such a child, they
came across the boy Merlin who was begot by supernatu-
ral means on a human mother.

When Merlin was brought to Dinas Emrys, he revealed
that the foundations were being built upon a subterranean
pool of water. Merlin also told the king that two flat stones
lay beneath the water and, beneath the stones, were two
dragons, one red and one white. The pressure of the materials for Vortigern's tower was making them uncomfortable and they were fighting each other. Merlin explained
that the red dragon symbolised the Britons and the white
dragon, the Saxons. The Saxons or English had driven the
British out of their own territories but they themselves
would be eventually driven back into the sea. The leader
who would achieve this would, of course, be King Arthur.
Merlin told Vortigern to build his tower on another site and
his life was spared because of his prophetic abilities. King
Arthur himself is known as Arthur 'Pendragon' which
comes from the Welsh 'pen', meaning 'head', thus indicat-

ing that he is the high king or the most important leader.

In Nordic mythology a giant dragon called Nidhoggr lives in the Underworld, coiled around the roots of the great world tree Yggdrasil that holds up the universe. Nidhoggr gnaws relentlessly at these roots and it is said that, should he bite through them, the world will be destroyed. Interestingly, the destructive energies of the dragon are countered in Norse myth by the Norns, who have Otherworld powers and heal the tree each day by bringing water to it from a well with magical properties. Once again in mythology, the dragon is linked in some way to water. As in the Golden Legend, mention is made of a source of healing water. In this case, it is a well; in the story of St George, it is the spring that issues from the altar of the church dedicated to the Blessed Virgin.

It has been suggested that a belief in the existence of dragons might stem from some dimly held collective memory of dinosaurs. However, the appearance of the first humans and the disappearance of the dinosaurs are events separated by a colossal 60 or 70 million years. Yet, although vast periods of time passed between the era of the dinosaurs and the arrival of humans, it is indisputable that people discovered their remains in the form of fossilised bones and footprints. No doubt, such discoveries would have influenced and, in some cases, generated myths and legends about dragons and other creatures. In many respects, however, the dragon, in its multitudinous forms, can also be interpreted as a projection of human fears, both real and imagined. Conversely, dragons have in some cases been regarded as lucky, fortuitous and been linked with prosperity and material wealth.

Dragons are an important and ancient part of Chinese culture and are often associated with elemental natural forces such as water, air, earth and fire. Chinese emperors claimed to be descended from dragons and their symbolism is particularly linked to festivities and rituals that celebrate and greet the coming of the season of spring. Chinese dragons are said to live exceptionally long lives – indeed, they are sometimes thought of as immortal. As in many of the myths that have so far been mentioned, Chinese dragons are alleged to have power over rain and the flow of water and, in this sense, are thought to help people. They are linked to fertility and often seen as having immense wisdom. The dragon is also one of the creatures of the Chinese horoscope. The qualities attributed to a person born under this sign provide an insight into how the Chinese view of the dragon often differs from Western interpretations. Dragon people are said to be flamboyant, energetic, original and lucky. In marked contrast to its often negative portrayal in later European traditions, the dragon brings good fortune and is respected, honoured and associated with authority.

Given that dragons are often equated with the coming of spring, with fertility and with sexual energy, it is perhaps not surprising that, in a number of medieval Christian paintings, the dragon that St George is fighting is shown to have female sexual organs. Within this Christian context, lust is something to be controlled and defeated and St

George emerges as a champion of chastity and purity. In one illustration of St George from 'Hours of the Virgin' (c.1430), held in the Bodleian Library, the dragon is shown lying on its back and being speared in the mouth. The dragon is lying in an attitude of sexual vulnerability and has female genitals and its anus is exposed. The psychology of this image and other depictions of a gendered dragon are not accidental and Samantha Riches has commented that 'the presence of external female genitalia in these images defines the dragon in quite a specific way, both as an obscene creature and also, crucially in her relationship to St George. A complex paradigm is set up of an act of penetration by the aggressive male which overthrows the sexuality of the female (he refuses to have actual coition with her) and at the same time sublimates his own sexual desires'. (Samantha Riches, *St George, Hero, Martyr and Myth*, p.171)

In other images of the late medieval period, the dragon is shown to have male genitals and the anus is clearly visible. Such images also imply the base animalistic qualities of the dragon, which St George is overcoming. These pictures may also allude to the medieval view of homosexuality as evil and obscene. The gendered dragon is comparatively unusual in the overall canon of representations of St George but illustrates the flexibility of meaning that his cult has demonstrated over time. The female dragon presents a complex psychological manifestation of medieval thought. As Samantha Riches observes, 'we must be careful not to see St George's monster simply as female. Rather she stands for a specific type of femininity that is sexual and bestial, everything that is worst about women to the late medieval mind.' (Samantha Riches, *St George, Hero, Martyr and Myth*, p.177)

In Russian and Greek icons of St George slaying the dragon, the dragon is often shown as a relatively small, almost dog-like creature. The artists are more concerned with emphasising the stature and power of St George and his role as a victorious champion of God. In these depictions, the power of 'good' is overwhelming and St George's victory is conclusive. In one English representation of the battle rendered in glass, from Leicester and dated to 1505, the dragon is twining its serpentine tail around the leg of the saint. This dragon also has another head on the end of the tail and St George's victory here appears to be altogether more hard-earned than in the Eastern traditions. In Greek iconic depictions of St George he is usually dressed in the armour of a Roman soldier. He is often accompanied by a 'cup-bearer' who is a much smaller figure, often seated behind George on the saint's horse. Perhaps unsurprisingly, he has more Mediterranean features and characteristics, such as olive skin and dark curly hair, reflecting his most likely origins in the near East.

As we have seen, the concept of a titanic struggle between a mythical monster or dragon and dragon-slayer is an extremely ancient one. However, its meaning and significance have undergone radical changes and re-interpretations, from the earliest creation myths to the dualistic conflict between good and evil that the story of George and the dragon represents. The legend of St George and the dragon itself has also proved open to considerable flexibility in interpretation. At different times, and in different images, it can be seen as symbolising the subjugation of pagan beliefs by the Christian church, the suppression of heretical movements, the battle over Christian sexual morals and the ultimate victory of Christ over the devil.

Mythological Heroes

As we have seen, a belief in dragons is an ancient and seemingly multi-cultural concept that reaches back to the earliest recorded times. The influence of such beliefs and myths on the story of St George's conflict with the dragon is apparent. However, it is the great heroes of Greek myth and legend who have most recognisably and directly influenced the story of St George. It is important to undertake a closer examination of these pre-Christian tales that bear striking similarities to the legend of George and the dragon. They also reveal striking differences between pagan and Christian ideals and values, and demonstrate the apparently universal need for heroes.

The Greek myth of Perseus and Andromeda has been thought by many to have exerted the greatest influence over the story of St George. Perseus was the son of Zeus, the father of the Greek Gods. His mother was called Danae and she was the daughter of Acrisius the king of Argos. An oracle had told Acrisius that he would be killed by the son of Danae and, in fear of this prophecy, he had his daughter locked away so that no man could make her pregnant. But the god Zeus desired her and changed his form into a shower of golden rain so that he could enter her prison through the gaps in its walls, and thus he conceived a child with her. (In Greek mythology there are numerous examples of Zeus desiring mortal women and changing his shape in the pursuit of his lust. In one story Zeus changes his shape to that of a bull and carries the beautiful Europa away to Crete to have intercourse with her and, in another, he transforms himself into a swan in order to seduce the Spartan Queen, Leda.) When Danae gave birth to Perseus, King Acrisius had them placed in a chest and cast out to sea, so fearful was he that the prophecy of his own death would come true. The chest was directed by the wind to the rocky island of Serifos, which was known as 'the barren one'. A fisherman called Dictys set them free and gave them shelter. The king of Serifos, Polydectes, desired Danae and wanted to marry her. When Perseus had reached adulthood he was invited to a banquet held by Polydectes and, in order to try to impress the king, claimed that he would carry out any task that he was set. He even stated that he would bring Polydectes the head of the terrifying monster Medusa, whose gaze could turn mortal men to stone, if the king wished it. Polydectes took Perseus up on his boast and said that, if he failed to bring him the head of the Gorgon, he would marry Danae with or without her consent.

A surviving frieze from the Temple of Artemis on Corfu gives a vivid depiction of how the ancient Greeks imagined Medusa. The Gorgon frieze, dating from the sixth century BC, portrays her as a terrifying monster with snakes growing from her head and a broad flat nose and teeth, modelled on those of a wild boar. Snakes encircle her waist and she is shown running upon winged sandals. With her association with serpents and her frightening appearance, Medusa can be seen to embody many dragon-like qualities.

In order to kill Medusa, Perseus needed the help of the nymphs and was assisted in his quest to find them by the god Hermes and the goddess Athena. They directed him to the Graiae, three old women who shared one eye and a single tooth between them. Perseus tricked them into relinquishing the eye and the tooth and used them to make the sisters tell him how to find the nymphs. The nymphs equipped him with gifts to aid him in his task – a magic helmet that made him invisible, a bag to hold the severed head of Medusa and a pair of winged sandals. Perseus travelled by sea to the place where Medusa and her sisters Euryale and Stheno lived. The sisters, known as the Gorgons, were fast asleep when Perseus arrived. He put on the magic helmet and the winged sandals and, following the advice of Athena, viewed the face of Medusa in the reflective metal of his shield so that he would not be turned to stone. Then he cut off Medusa's head and placed it in the bag given to him by the nymphs. In death, Medusa gave birth to the winged horses Pegasus and Chrysaor, who sprang from her neck and whose father was Poseidon, god of the seas. Perseus carried away the head of Medusa and escaped the remaining two Gorgon sisters. According to the myth, drops of blood fell from the head of Medusa as Perseus travelled through Africa and produced wild animals that populated the country.

When Perseus reached the coast, he happened upon a beautiful girl who was chained to a stone just as St George met the princess in the *Golden Legend*. He discovered that the girl, whose name was Andromeda, was intended as a sacrifice to a terrible sea monster. Cassiope, the mother of Andromeda, had angered the Nymphs by claiming that her daughter was more beautiful than them. As punishment, they persuaded Poseidon to unleash a great flood upon the country of Andromeda and to unleash a terrible sea monster upon the people. An oracle advised King Cepheus, Andromeda's father, that he would have to offer his child as a sacrifice to appease the creature. Just as in the myth of St George and the dragon, Perseus resolves to kill the monster and save the beautiful girl. However, Perseus agrees to do this on the condition that King Cepheus lets him marry Andromeda, should he succeed. (In the various re-tellings of the story of St George, he sometimes marries the princess but, in the *Golden Legend*, he does not. More emphasis is placed on the conversion of the pagan people to Christianity than to the romance inherent in the story.) Perseus kills the sea creature but Cepheus reneges upon their agreement. Perseus punishes him by showing him the head of Medusa and turning him to stone. Andromeda and Perseus travel back to Serifos where King Polydectes breaks his promise and is also turned to stone.

Interestingly, once Perseus has completed his quest, the fisherman Dictys then becomes king of the land. In the legends of the Holy Grail, the wounded fisher king is restored and healed when the quest knight Perceval (usually by the asking of a ritual question) achieves the Grail. There are obvious parallels here, both in the names of the heroes and in the idea of a fisher king whose destiny is determined by the successful resolution of a difficult task or quest.

It is worth noting that the legend of Perseus has a tragic ending, just as, some would argue, the martyrdom of St George does. Following the death of Polydectes, Perseus travels back to his original homeland of Argos to look for his grandfather King Acrisius. News reaches Acrisius of the approach of Perseus and he is reminded of the oracle that told him the son of his daughter Danae would end his life. Acrisius flees to the land of Larisa, which is ruled by King Tentamides. By a strange twist of fate Tentamides holds games in which Perseus participates. Whilst throwing the discus, Perseus misses his target and strikes Acrisius a terrible blow to the head. He discovers that he has killed his grandfather and, overwhelmed with great sorrow, accords him a magnificent funeral.

Some sources claim that Perseus slew the sea monster in Palestine. The places often suggested as the site of the battle are the towns of Joppa and Arsuf, which are very close to Lydda where St George is alleged to have been buried. Some scholars have argued that this pre-Christian myth became attached to the figure of George and there are clearly many striking similarities. Once again, the monster is linked to water. George's dragon lives in a lake and Perseus's beast in the sea. Perhaps crusaders in the Holy Land heard the story of Perseus and linked his bravery to that of St George. Richard the Lionheart is said to have discovered the tomb of St George at Lydda during fighting in the Third Crusade between 1191 and 1192.

The story of Theseus and the Minotaur also has curious parallels to the legend of St George. The myth of Theseus and the Minotaur begins when Theseus kills a Cretan bull that is causing devastation in Marathon. Poseidon had created the bull as a gift to King Minos of Crete but, when the king refused to sacrifice it, the god maddened the animal so that it ran wild on the island. As part of his labours Heracles was set the task of capturing it alive and bringing it to Mycenae on the Greek mainland. He accomplished his task but the bull was later set free and again ran wild. Theseus captures the bull and sacrifices it to Apollo in the city of Athens. Previously, Androgeos, the son of King Minos, had attempted to kill the bull but he had failed and the animal killed him. Enraged by Theseus's triumph where his son failed, Minos punishes the Athenians terribly. They are ordered to send as tribute to Crete every nine years a boat filled with seven maidens and seven youths. These are to be fed to the terrible Minotaur, the offspring of the Cretan bull and Pasiphae, the wife of King Minos, which has a human body and the head of a bull and feasts on human flesh. Theseus bravely offers to rid Athens of the need to pay this sickening tribute and travels with the boat full of youths and maidens to Crete. Theseus promises his father that, if he is successful and kills the Minotaur, he will sail back to Athens with white sails instead of the black ones his ship carries in grief and mourning for the tribute to Minos. The king of Crete travels on the boat himself as he wants to oversee the transport of the youth of Athens himself. When he makes advances on one of the Athenian girls Theseus is angered and intervenes, telling Minos that he is the son of Poseidon. To test the truth of his claim Minos throws a ring into the sea and suggests Theseus prove his divine parenthood by seeking the aid of Poseidon to recover it. Theseus leaps overboard and, whilst Zeus hurls a bolt of lightning to illuminate his way, he is assisted by Poseidon to travel to the depths of the sea to find the ring. He fulfils the challenge and is returned to the boat by Poseidon, wearing dry clothes but holding the ring.

At least two themes emerge from this story that echo St George's legend. There is the motif of the youth of a city being terrorised by a man-eating monster and that of a central hero who undertakes to rid the people of the creature and who is favoured in this endeavour by divine intervention.

When Theseus reaches Crete, the goddess Aphrodite uses her powers to make Ariadne, the daughter of King Minos, fall in love with him and aid him in his task. It is Ariadne who gives Theseus a ball of thread when he enters the labyrinth, the maze of tunnels beneath the Palace of Minos where the Minotaur lives. By unwinding the thread as he goes through the passages and corridors of the labyrinth, Theseus will be able to make his way back out again.

Finally he reaches the Minotaur and, after a violent struggle, he kills it. Making his escape Theseus flees Crete with Ariadne and the crew of his ship. (Interestingly, as in some versions of the St George story, the hero does not marry the princess. Theseus is said to stop off at the island of Naxos where he leaves Ariadne.) Travelling in haste back to Athens to celebrate his victory, Theseus forgets to change the sails on board his ship. When his father sees the boat of Theseus returning with black sails, he hurls himself from the Acropolis, thinking his son has been killed. So the story ends in tragedy, just as the story of George ends in the saint's martyrdom.

In the legend of Jason and the Golden Fleece there are two references to dragons in tasks which the hero must perform. Jason is the son of Polymela whose father was King Cretheus of Iolcus. Following the death of Cretheus, Pelias, the half-brother of Polymela, becomes king because he is the child of Poseidon and the queen of Iolcus. Jason is entrusted to the care of the centaur Chiron, half man and half horse, to keep the boy safe from Pelias who jealously guards his throne. An oracle has previously told Pelias that, one day, he will lose his kingdom to a youth with one sandal. When he has reached maturity Jason sets out for Iolcus to claim his kingship. On the way he helps an old woman to cross a stream and loses one of his sandals. The old woman is, in fact, the goddess Hera in disguise. When he arrives at the court of Pelias, the king sees he is only wearing one sandal and is terrified. Jason explains who he is and asks that Pelias pass the crown to him, telling Pelias that he can retain his wealth and belongings and need only abdicate. The king agrees to do so on the condition that Jason travels to the land of Colchis and fetches for him the

Golden Fleece that is kept there. Jason accepts the challenge. He has a boat built called the Argo and assembles a crew of heroes to sail her. The Argonauts, as they are called, include such luminaries of Greek myth as Heracles, Orpheus and Theseus.

After many adventures, the Argonauts reach Colchis and approach King Aeetes to request the Golden Fleece. Aeetes agrees to hand it over if Jason can complete two difficult tasks. His first task is to yoke together two dangerous bulls that breathe fire. His second is to sow dragon's teeth in a field and then fight the army that magically springs up from them. Jason accomplishes these challenges but only with the help of Medea, daughter of Aeetes, who is a sorceress. Aphrodite causes Eros to fire an arrow into the heart of Medea that makes her fall in love with Jason and she is compelled to aid him. But Aeetes breaks his promise and the Argonauts set out to steal the fleece. They find it in a sacred grove, hanging on a tree guarded by a huge dragon or serpent that threatens to kill any who approach it. Medea sends the dragon to sleep, in some versions of the tale by singing a lullaby and in others by using a sleeping potion. Jason seizes the fleece and carries it to Iolcus, undergoing many adventures and trials on the return journey.

In one telling of the tale Jason became the king with the help of Medea. However, in another darker and more tragic version, Jason falls in love with another woman and Medea kills the children she and Jason have conceived. She then poisons the woman with whom Jason has fallen in love. Jason ends his days a friendless, childless old man who is finally killed when he is visiting the wreck of the Argo and the prow of the ship falls on him, crushing him to death.

Although the tale of Jason and the tale of St George evolved from two very different religious traditions, they share a number of common elements and both describe a hero who overcomes great obstacles and danger with divine intervention and favour. Although St George's story is set in a Christian context, it also displays magical elements such as the appearance of a dragon and the healing spring that flows from the altar of the church that George founds.

As part of the Twelve Labours of Heracles the hero must complete a set of difficult tasks set for him by King Eurytheus. For his second Labour Heracles has to destroy a terrible dragon which has nine heads and lives in a marsh close to the Argolic Gulf. The dragon has been feeding on the flocks of the local people and asphyxiating the population with its poisonous breath. Heracles finds the monster known as the Hydra lurking in a spring called Amymone and attacks it with his club. However, every time he destroys one of the monster's heads, two or three more grow back in its place. Eventually Heracles gives his faithful companion Iolaus the job of cauterising each stump with a flaming torch to stop them growing back. This plan succeeds and Heracles kills the Hydra. In a later adventure Heracles kills a dragon that has been causing destruction to the lands of Laomedon, the king of Troy. An oracle has told the king to tie his daughter, Hesione, to a rock as a sacrifice to the dragon. Heracles intervenes, slaying the dragon and releasing the princess.

Dragon- or monster-slaying heroes also occur frequently in the mythologies of Northern Europe, perhaps most famously in the story of Beowulf. In this saga, a terrible monster called Grendel has been preying on the great hall of the Danes for twelve years, taking victims at night as they sleep and devouring them. Beowulf is a brave warrior of the Geats who undertakes to stop the monster and does so by tearing off the arm of Grendel and so killing it. The Danes celebrate the death of Grendel but they are unaware that the monster has a mother who attacks their hall in revenge the following night. Beowulf pursues the mother of Grendel to her lair in a local lake and dives in, eventually killing her with his sword. In time Beowulf becomes king and, years later, when a treasure-guarding dragon begins to terrorise the population, he undertakes to kill it. But Beowulf is older than when he faced Grendel and its mother and, although he succeeds in dispatching the dragon, he is mortally wounded in the battle and dies soon afterwards.

The Norse hero Siegfried, also called Sigurd, faces a dragon in order to gain the treasure it is guarding. Siegfried is the son of Sigmund who had been killed in battle by Odin, after striking the god. Sigmund willed the shattered fragments of his sword to his wife Hjordis, who was pregnant with Siegfried, as an heirloom. Hjordis married King Alf who then fostered Siegfried to Regin, one of the dwarves of Norse mythology. Regin encourages greed and resentment in Siegfried in order to manipulate him to perform a task for him.

When Regin mocks Siegfried for his position as a stable boy, Siegfried decides to get a horse for himself. He then meets a mysterious old man who is, in fact, the god Odin in disguise. The old man helps him select a horse that was bred from Odin's own wondrous steed Sleipnir. Regin tells Siegfried about the hoard of gold that his brother Fafnir has amassed by killing their father Hreidmar. Fafnir, inspired by his own greed, has transformed himself into the shape of a dragon in order to guard the gold. Regin persuades Siegfried to kill Fafnir so that they can claim the gold for themselves. The god Mimir helps Siegfried by re-forging the fragments of his father's sword. The name of the sword is Gram and it is strong enough to cut through the anvil on which it was made. Following the advice of Regin, Siegfried digs a pit in the ground that he covers. When Fafnir passes over it he stabs him in the belly and kills him. Odin, once again assuming the form of an old man, advises him to dig trenches to catch the blood of Fafnir and to bathe in it. This will make Siegfried invulnerable to harm. Siegfried follows his advice and bathes in the blood. It covers all of his body apart from the point on his shoulder where a leaf has stuck to him.

The dwarf Regin asks Siegfried for the heart of Fafnir but Siegfried has tasted the blood of Fafnir and this gives him the power to understand the language of the birds in the trees. The birds warn him that Regin intends to kill him so Siegfried cuts off Regin's head. He then eats part of the heart of Fafnir himself and so gains the gift of prophecy. This Norse pagan myth of Siegfried slaying Fafnir also found its way into Christian culture. It was often portrayed in Scandinavian churches where the dragon Fafnir, of course, came to symbolise the devil, overcome by Siegfried – another representation of the power of good over evil. Siegfried's greed for gold, however, contrasts with the behaviour of St George who, in the stories attached to him, refuses material reward for the prize of converting pagans to Christianity. The myth of Siegfried echoes both the story of King Arthur, whose sword Excalibur is drawn from an anvil, and the legend of Achilles, who is dipped in the waters of the river Styx by his mother and thus made invulnerable to attack. However, like Siegfried one spot on his body is untouched by the bathing – the ankle by which his mother held him. Eventually he is killed by a poisoned arrow shot into his ankle.

St George has also been linked to other pre-Christian traditions, notably that of the Green Man. This nature deity, who personifies growth, fertility and the coming of spring, is a strong part of English folk traditions and also has parallels in many other cultures. The Green Man not only gives his name to many English pubs (as does St George) but is often found carved in wood and stone in churches, particularly in images dating from the medieval period. Because St George's Day fell on 23 April, close to the coming of spring, he has long been associated with themes of renewal and fertility. In Greece, 'Agios Georgios', 'St George's Day', is amongst the most important feast days in the calendar of the Orthodox Church, where he is considered the patron saint of shepherds. His feast day marks the start of the grazing season for farmers. Through his own name, which derives from the Greek word for farmer, he is the patron saint of farmers but also, more specifically, husbandmen. Indeed, as Christopher Stace has observed, 'St George's day traditionally marks the beginning of spring sowing' (Christopher Stace, *St George, Patron Saint of England,* p.62). The Green Man of pre-Christian myth has even been referred to as 'Green George', demonstrating the way in which the roles of these two important figures became intertwined over time.

As well as being clearly linked to themes of growth and re-birth, St George has had a powerful reputation as a healing saint. In the *Golden Legend* a healing spring miraculously appears in the altar of the church that the saint founds. St George has been invoked against a range of diseases including leprosy, syphilis, the plague, herpes and skin rashes. It has been argued that he was called upon for help with these particular illnesses because he himself had defeated the dragon with its scaled skin and pestilential breath.

St George also appears to have links with an Islamic hero known as Al Khidr whose name means the 'Green One'. Al Khidr is said to have discovered the fountain of youth and, by drinking from its waters, he attained immortality. When he drank from its waters his skin, clothes and even his footsteps became a vivid blue green colour. In the Koran he is described as a teacher who instructs Moses, perplexing him with a series of seemingly destructive and random acts, only to reveal in the end the divine pattern of meaning that informs them. In one story Al Khidr restores a fish to life by sprinkling sacred water upon it and, in another, battles a thousand armed demons. Interestingly, the tomb of St George at Lydda appears to have been a focus of devotion for Muslims as well as Christians and the similarities between the two figures may have influenced this. Al Khidr is known as a healing figure but also for acts of 'destruction' which are eventually seen as having positive outcomes. Al Khidr battles the demon just as George fought the dragon. His 'greenness' and regenerative powers also echo aspects of the cult of St George. Arab Christians thought that St George was the re-incarnation of Elijah and he is often referred to as 'Girgis' or 'Jirjis' in Coptic Churches. St George's Bay, near Beirut, is also claimed to be the place where St George killed the dragon, further emphasising his links to the Middle East.

Saint George and Medieval Warfare

Although there is evidence that St George was known and revered in England prior to 1066, his cult was particularly strong at this time in Normandy. By the late medieval period Normandy could boast nearly seventy churches dedicated in his honour as well as healing springs and a number of important local guilds. It was to be his popularity with the Norman invaders and his role within the crusades of the medieval period that would pave the way for his adoption by the English as their patron saint.

One particular event that took place in Normandy during the eighth century seems to have greatly influenced the link between the saint and the region. One source, writing at the time of a certain Austrulph, an abbot in Normandy from 743 AD to 753 AD, records that a mysterious container was washed ashore at Portbail in Normandy. When the casket, said to have been shaped like a lighthouse, was opened, those present discovered, to their amazement, a finely made copy of the gospels in Latin, a piece of the true cross and various relics from a number of saints. Most importantly, in this context, it contained a reliquary that held a piece of the jawbone of St George.

Intriguingly, each item was accompanied by a letter of authentication. The provenance of these treasures has been the cause of much speculation, both at the time and since. Perhaps they were being transported by sea and were involved in some kind of maritime disaster. For the people of the Cotentin area in Normandy, it must have seemed like some form of divine intervention. Records state that the local leaders once again decided to let the hand of God direct where these items should be placed. The container was loaded onto a cart pulled by oxen and the people allowed the animals to wander freely. When the oxen stopped at a town called Brix, the governor of Cotentin, Count Richwin decided to build a church to house the items there. As well as a church dedicated to St George, two other buildings were erected which were dedicated to the Blessed Virgin and the Holy Cross.

Some writers have claimed that William the Conqueror himself fought under the Red Cross flag of St George during the invasion of Anglo-Saxon England. More reliably, William of Malmesbury records that the army of Robert II, Duke of Normandy and son of William, had St George as its patron saint when it fought in the First Crusade which began in 1095. A number of Norman churches in England are either dedicated to St George or contain images of him in which he is very often depicted as a mounted knight. The church at Fordington in Dorset, dating from 1100, which has already been mentioned in Chapter Three, merits closer attention. The carving of St George at Fordington shows the saint aiding the Christian army fighting at the battle of

Antioch during the First Crusade. On one side of the carved stone panel the Christian soldiers are shown kneeling in prayer looking up at St George who is spearing an enemy soldier through the mouth. The soldier is falling back onto the bodies of his fallen comrades whom George has already killed. A flag displaying a cross on it flies from the lance of St George and his head appears to be surrounded by a halo. Interestingly, it is has been noted that the only way the Muslim and Christian troops can be separated visually is by their differing shield types. The Muslim troops carry round shields and this became a common visual device in art from this period. In this carving both sets of soldiers appear otherwise to be modelled on Norman troops with chain mail garments and a distinctive pointed helmet with a small metal bar to protect the nose.

The Battle of Antioch took place in 1098 and was an important and, in many ways, miraculous victory for the Christian crusaders. It is therefore important to consider in greater detail the circumstances and events of this battle and, specifically, the role it has played in developing the legend of St George. The ancient city of Antioch had a special significance for the crusaders because of its important links to early Christianity. Today, the ruins of the classical city are located near the small town of Antakya in Turkey, close to the Syrian border. In 1098, the majority of the population of the town were, in fact, Christians who were ruled over by Turkish Muslims. St Peter had preached in Antioch and the very word 'Christian' had first been used in the city. St Peter and his followers had been persecuted for their religious beliefs and had held services in secret. A cave known as St Peter's Grotto still exists today on Mount Silpius, an area actually surrounded by the walls of the old city, where Peter and his followers are said to have worshipped.

The crusader army reached Antioch in the autumn of 1097 after a difficult and dangerous overland journey across Asia Minor. Not only was Antioch a city of religious and spiritual importance but, because of its proximity to the port of St Symeon and the coastal region, it also held strategic and military value. On arrival, the crusading army, which was made up of a combined force of mainly French or Frankish groups, was led by a variety of Christian princes and nobles. They laid siege to the city while the different factions quarrelled about the best way to overcome the Muslim defenders. The mountainous location and the fact that the city walls ran for some eighteen miles made Antioch a particularly difficult stronghold to breach. Because the walls also enclosed gardens and pastures, the defenders could not easily be starved out. In fact, it was to be the crusaders themselves who were to suffer from lack of provisions and many are thought to have starved from lack of food. Some began to desert before the arrival of an English fleet bolstered their supplies and resolve. Eventually, a traitor within the Antioch garrison agreed to let the crusaders in at night by lowering a ladder from the city walls. A group of knights entered in this way and then let in the main crusading army through the gates of the city. The soldiers destroyed the garrison and Armenian

Christians sympathetic to the cause of the crusaders beheaded the Turkish governor. The capture of Antioch was particularly timely because a much larger, better-provisioned Turkish army led by Kerbogha was on its way to assist the beleaguered garrison. Many crusaders left the city after its capture, fearful of the oncoming forces of Kerbogha, and the previously sympathetic Byzantine Emperor withdrew an offer of aid. The Christian army in Antioch was depleted in numbers and in a sorry state. Those that remained were weakened by hunger and many were suffering from disease and illness. The future for the crusaders at Antioch looked grim but their spirits were lifted by a peasant called Peter Bartholomew who claimed to have been visited in a vision by St Andrew.

In the vision the saint had informed Peter of the whereabouts within Antioch of the actual spear that had been used to pierce the side of Jesus Christ at the crucifixion. A priest in the crusader army also claimed to have been visited by Christ himself who told him that they would be given divine assistance. These visions helped lift the morale of the Christian army and an excavation of the Cathedral of St Peter was undertaken to find the holy lance. Peter Bartholomew himself appeared to find the lance in a pit dug into the floor of the cathedral, although some later disputed this supposed 'miracle'. Nonetheless, the discovery of the lance greatly revived the Christian forces. Peter proclaimed that the ghosts of their fallen comrades would join them in their battle and that saints and angels would swell their numbers. Whipping themselves into a religious fever, the crusaders voluntarily fasted and spent days immersed in prayer and ritual, calling on God to protect them in their darkest hour. A decision was reached to open the city gates and to lead a charge against the much larger and stronger Muslim army of Kerbogha. Their bishops and priests urged on the crusaders who, through lack of food, had been reduced to chewing boiled bark. The holy lance itself was carried into battle and the crusaders believed that a spectral army led by St George attacked Kerbogha's forces from the nearby hills. St George was also said to have been accompanied in his charge against the Turks by St Maurice, St Theodore and St Demetrius and other important soldier saints of the early Christian era. Miraculously, the Muslim army began to turn and flee and the crusaders drove them from the field. In the potent atmosphere of religious fervour, and perhaps suffering from the effects of near starvation, the crusaders claimed that the saints and an army of the ghosts of fallen knights had saved them. A more mundane explanation, offered by historians, is that the crusaders benefited from divisions in the Turkish forces and that quarrelling leaders were unwilling to support Kerbogha for fear it would undermine their own power.

Following the victory at Antioch the crusader army eventually moved south to Palestine and the sacred city of Jerusalem which, at this time, was controlled by Egyptian Muslims. Jerusalem, scene of the death and resurrection of Jesus, was regarded in the Middle Ages as the most sacred centre for pilgrimage and worship in the world. Because of its impressive fortifications, it was also a daunting prospect for any invading army. Whereas Antioch contained many sympathetic to the crusaders, the Egyptian rulers of Jerusalem had expelled all Christians from the city before their arrival. Provisions and water once again became serious problems for the crusaders when they arrived at Jerusalem on 7 June 1099. All the local fields had been laid bare, cattle removed and wells had been filled in or corrupted. A hermit whom the leaders of the Christian army met on the Mount of Olives advised them to attack at once. They followed his advice but the attempt to take the city failed. Once again, many crusaders began to desert their army and morale sank in the face of the well-defended city and the prospect of an army of Egyptians marching from Cairo to engage with them. However, a priest of the pilgrim army had a vision that the crusaders should march barefoot around the walls of the city, repent their sins and fast. If they did so, God would grant them victory against the Infidels. The crusaders probably numbered around 15,000 at this point and they began a procession around the perimeter walls of Jerusalem. The priests at the head of the procession carried with them the holy lance found at Antioch, as well as other precious relics, including a reliquary holding the arm bone of St George that had been carried to the Holy Land from a Byzantine monastery.

When ships from England and Italy arrived on the coast, the crusaders received much needed supplies and reinforcements. Robert of Normandy, who had placed his army under the protection of St George, was amongst those besieging the city. Huge towers were built to scale the city walls and these were used in conjunction with battering rams to force a way into Jerusalem. Those in the siege towers managed to leap onto the battlements on 15 July 1099 and began opening the city gates. Many of the defenders fled in terror and the attackers were able to clamber up ladders and breach the defences of the city. It was claimed that St George himself, leading a heavenly army, aided the crusaders at the siege of Jerusalem and that he was wearing a suit of white armour bearing the Red Cross symbol. Less inspiring, if unsurprising, was the massacre by the Christian army of those Jewish and Muslim inhabitants who remained in the city. But for the crusaders their most important objective had been reached. They had control over Jerusalem and sacred sites such as the Holy Sepulchre where it was said the body of Christ had been laid after his death.

Frescoes executed between 1080 and 1120 at St Botolph's church in Hardham, Sussex appear to record the appearance of St George at the Battle of Antioch and also show other episodes from his life and martyrdom. A carving at Damerham in Hampshire from 1100 show the saint trampling an enemy under the hooves of his horse. He is holding aloft a sword and carrying an identifiably Norman shield that tapers to a point at its base. The image of St George in these representations is one of a Norman horseman or 'chevalier' who fights a clearly human enemy. He emerges as a firmly martial figure, unforgiving in battle. There is little suggestion of the chivalrous knight that St George has come to exemplify today. These carvings reveal the values and attitudes of the Norman culture that created them.

Further evidence of St George's role in Norman England is provided by the church dedicated to him in the town of Clun in Shropshire, close to the Welsh border. The church tower of St George's is a squat, heavily fortified building and it is thought that, before the completion of the nearby Norman castle, it may have provided a secure point of defence against the marauding Welsh. In this context St George, anticipating his role in later centuries, emerges as a strongly militaristic saint, invoked in defence of the 'English' against a foreign enemy. Further north, in Shrewsbury, a town set in a loop of the river Severn, the nearest bridge to Wales is known as the Welsh Bridge. It is interesting that, during the middle ages, it was known as St George's Bridge and that, in all likelihood, a chapel dedicated to the saint stood nearby. A Norman castle was built in Shrewsbury to protect against the incursions made by Welsh armies and the town has been the scene of numerous conflicts between the two nations. It seems likely that the naming of the bridge in honour of the soldier saint demonstrates the emerging role of St George as a special protector of the English.

Back in the Middle East, the defeat of Christian forces at the battle of Hattin in 1187 plunged the crusader-occupied territories into chaos as the Muslim leader Saladin systematically overwhelmed them. Saladin's military success precipitated a Third Crusade that followed in the wake of a disastrous Second Crusade. Following the defeat at Hattin,

Western leaders, including King Henry II of England and King Philip of France, answered the Pope's plea for a new crusade. Both kings took vows to defend the Holy Land and, in order to finance their military expeditions, raised a tax called the Saladin Tithe. Ironically, plans for the crusade had to be put on hold when war erupted between the two countries. Richard the Lionheart, who was the son of Henry II, joined forces with Philip and challenged his own father. When Henry II died in 1189, Richard became king of England. Although Richard the Lionheart has a reputation as a glorious English king he only spent a mere six months of his ten-year reign in the country.

He was crowned in Westminster Abbey and, after raising considerable sums from England and from his lands in Northern and Western France, he set off almost immediately on the new crusade. Richard's journey to the Holy Land began by travelling across France to the port of Marseilles. From there he went to Sicily and then his assembled fleet set sail for Acre, calling at the island of Rhodes on the way. However, a number of his ships had been caught up in a storm that forced them onto the coast of Cyprus. Richard came into conflict with the self-proclaimed 'Emperor of Cyprus', Isaac Ducas Comnenus, who had claimed Richard's ships and goods. Richard demanded them back. When the Emperor refused, Richard quickly overthrew him and captured Cyprus. He had originally planned to marry his fiancée Princess Berengaria, the daughter of King Sancho of Navarre, when his army reached Palestine. However, following his conquest of

Cyprus, he married her in the chapel of St George at Limassol on 12 May 1191. Whether or not this can be regarded as evidence of Richard's special reverence for the cult of St George is hard to say but, in view of the links made between the king and the saint, it is nonetheless an interesting detail. On reaching the Holy Land, Richard is alleged to have had a vision of St George during the siege of Acre in that same year. As mentioned in Chapter Four, legend states that Richard visited the tomb of St George at Lydda and sought his patronage. He may also have been responsible for re-building a cathedral on the site of the tomb that Saladin had destroyed. There have been claims that Richard's troops flew the flag of St George but the first unequivocal reference to the English army using his banner is during the reign of Edward I. In 1277, when the English army under Edward were fighting the Welsh, it is recorded that they flew the arms of St George. These banners were also displayed alongside those of St Edmund and St Edward the Confessor.

The unique and unusual carvings found in Royston Cave in Cambridgeshire testify to the significance and popularity of St George in the years after the crusades. Royston Cave was created by the Knights Templar, the order of warrior monks, originally formed in 1119 with the intention of protecting pilgrims travelling though the Holy Land. The cave is believed to have been a secret meeting place for Templars who owned land and properties in the area. The Templars were extremely powerful and influential, gaining land and wealth through the patronage of the nobility and aristocracy across Europe. Legally, they were answerable only to the Pope himself and their autonomy coupled with their wealth led to a great deal of jealousy towards the order. Following the fall of Acre to the Muslim forces in 1291, the Templars lost both popularity and support. Terrible accusations of heresy were made against them and, on Friday 13 October 1307, King Philip IV of France arrested and tortured many members of the order. By 1312, the order had been suppressed by the then Pope Clement V. It is during this period of persecution and repression that Royston Cave is thought to have been created.

Dug out of the chalk layer that the town of Royston is built on, the cave is believed to have served as both a secret meeting point and a place of initiation and religious ritual for members of the order. The walls of the cave are crowded with an astonishing array of carvings that depict a variety of religious subject matter, from the crucifixion to portrayals of St Katherine, St Lawrence and St Christopher. Pagan images such as a Sheila-na-gig and a horse are carved alongside symbols that are seemingly peculiar to the Templars, such as a hand with a heart on it and a series of four concentric circles. St George, wearing armour with a cross on the breastplate and pointing his sword at a long line of figures, is a major presence in the carvings. The figures at which George is pointing are thought to be the twelve disciples with Jesus. Judas appears as a small figure in the carving at the right. Sylvia Beamon has argued that the symbolic value of St George in this context is that he 'rescues the lady (that is the church) from the devil or the oppressor, represented by the dragon' (quoted in Peter T Houldcroft, *A Pictorial Guide to Royston Cave*, p.8). Perhaps the order saw St George as a figure of protection at this terrible time in its own history. The Templars also believed that St George had appeared at the battle of Ramleh on 25 November 1177, where they had defeated the forces of Saladin. St George was believed to have ridden his horse next to the king of Jerusalem who was dying. Conservation work in 1996–1997 revealed that the carving of St George also had a socket in its left hip and that he probably would have had a wooden lance held in it that would have been attached to a wooden platform within the chamber. St George is, of course, the patron saint of knights.

However, the popularity of St George as we have seen was not merely limited to England during the Middle Ages. His popularity grew amongst many Christian regions and nations. During the 'Reconquista' of Spain, St George is said to have helped defeat the Moors at the Battle of Alcoraz in 1095. He also made an appearance at the Battle of Puig in 1237 and was an important figure in the crusade against the Muslim forces. In 1352 St George or 'Sant Jordi' was declared patron saint of Catalonia in Northern Spain. On his feast day of 23 April, it is customary for Catalonian men to give women red roses and for the women to give the men books in return as gifts. It seems likely that this reflects George's identification in the medieval period with the concept of chivalrous behaviour towards women. Interestingly, the Spanish author Cervantes died on St

George's Day in 1616. Cervantes, of course, is best known for his creation of the comic character Don Quixote who famously tilted at windmills. His works are also celebrated on the feast of Sant Jordi.

In Germany, Henry II made him patron of his nobles and in 1015 the choir of Bamberg Cathedral was dedicated in his name. On St George's Day 1245, the Hohenstaufen Emperor Frederick II founded an order of knights who marched under the banner of St George. Other German rulers such as Frederick IV and Maximilian I belonged to Orders of St George. He has been claimed as patron saint of Germany and also counted as one of the 'fourteen holy helpers', a group of saints revered in the Rhineland from the fourth century AD onwards. Their popularity was, in part, due to their individual reputations as powerful intercessors against disease – further evidence of the link between St George and healing.

Images of St George can be found in churches in south western France, dating from the time of the Hundred Years War (1337–1453), when the English had considerable influence and control in the region. In the church of St Foy (Faith) in the medieval town of Pujols near Villeneuve Sur Lot, fifteenth century frescoes of St George fighting the dragon can still be seen today. Similarly, at the tiny woodland church of Eglise de Notre Dame de Saux near Cahors in the Quercy region, frescoes survive from the fourteenth century which depict St George as a crusader knight, spearing the dragon in the mouth. The wall paintings at Saux clearly portray St George bearing the Red Cross arms with which he is associated on his shield and tabard and on the livery of his charger. The church also contains a fresco of the life of St Katherine. The nearby city of Cahors lies on an important pilgrimage route to Santiago de Compostela in north western Spain. It would also have been one route for English crusaders and pilgrims travelling from Bordeaux overland to the port of Marseilles from where they would have embarked for the Holy Land.

The Patron Saint of England

It was during the reign of Edward III that the link between St George and English royalty was most firmly established. Edward was king between 1327 and 1377 and there is ample evidence of his own particular veneration of the saint. A document known as the Milemete Treatise has survived from the beginning of his reign which gives a fascinating insight into the new king's role. It was presented to Edward by Master Walter of Milemete around 1326 or 1327 and was intended to give advice and instruction on his duties and responsibilities as king. Master Walter was the King's Clerk and occupied a very significant and senior role in Edward's court. The treatise contains illustrations of Edward III being presented with his arms by St George himself. Both the king and the saint are depicted wearing armour and Edward is holding a lance whilst St George hands him a shield bearing the new king's coat of arms. St George is wearing a tabard that features his own red cross whilst Edward's displays his own coat of arms. In this instance, St George is presented as the embodiment of the chivalrous knight and it is to this pinnacle of virtue and bravery that Edward must aspire. The special relationship between Edward and St George is also reflected in wall paintings from St Stephen's chapel in the palace of Westminster that showed the monarch and his male relatives being led to the high altar by St George. The paintings have subsequently been lost but fortunately they were copied and their iconography recorded. Edward is also known to have possessed a container that was said to hold some of the blood of St George. Significantly, Edward is recorded as calling on the aid of the saint during the siege of Calais in 1349, a military encounter at which the English were victorious.

However, Edward's most dramatic statement of his devotion to St George was in his formation of the Order of the Garter in 1348. Edward and his son the Black Prince, who each led two groups of twelve knights, headed the Order. The Knights of the Order of the Garter were amongst the most powerful and influential figures of their time and the values of the organisation stressed chivalrous behaviour and complete loyalty to the king. Edward made St George's Chapel at Windsor Castle the centre of the order. St George's Chapel was actually an extension of an existing building which had originally been dedicated to St Edward the Confessor. However, the importance of St George to Edward meant that the significance of the Confessor rapidly diminished. The order was originally dedicated to the Virgin Mary, St George and St Edward the Confessor but, almost immediately, St George emerged as the most important of the three in the king's esteem. It is known that the chapel was filled with representations of St

George, including a statue of George and the dragon, and a reliquary that contained a number of the saint's bones. Much has been lost but numerous images of St George survive in the form of carvings within the chapel which show his life and martyrdom. Of particular note was the creation of an alabaster reredos for the high altar that also probably featured the life of the saint. It is known that ten carts were required to move the various panels of which it consisted. Ten horses drew each cart and it was transported from Nottingham, where it was made, to the chapel at Windsor.

The inaugural ceremony of the Order of the Garter took place on St George's Day, 23 April. Why Edward chose the symbol of the Garter has been the cause of some contention. Some stories say that, one day, the king found the garter of his mistress or wife on the ground and picked it up whilst a number of laughing knights looked on. As a rebuke to the knights, he is said to have elevated the garter to the highest status at court by making it the insignia of his order. The motto of the Order of the Garter is 'Evil to him who thinks evil of it'. A great feast was held at Windsor to mark the commencement of the order and the knights who had sworn allegiance to it wore their ceremonial dress. A chronicler of the time called Geoffrey le Baker recorded that 'They were all clothed like the King in cloaks of russet powdered with garters, dark blue in colour, and also had similar garters on their right legs, with blue mantles bearing shields of the arms of St George... they sat at table together in honour of the holy martyr, from whom they took the title of this most noble brotherhood, calling the company of these men of "St George de la Gartiere"', (quoted in Richard Barber, *The Reign of Chivalry*, p166)

The red cross of St George was adopted by a number of English towns and cities during the Middle Ages. Most notably, it appears in the armorial bearings of London. St Paul, of course, is the patron saint of London but St George enjoyed a central and often prestigious position as patron of some of the most important guilds of the city. An early reference to the flag of the city occurs in relation to Robert Fitz-Walter, the Castellan of London. Before his death in 1235 he was presented with the banner of London by the Mayor and it is described as being 'of bright red, with a figure of Paul in gold, with the feet and hands and head in silver and a sword in the hand of the said figure' (CLRO Information Sheet 5, Corporation Of London Records Office). This represents the weapon with which St Paul was martyred and it can still be found today in the first quarter of the St George's cross on the arms of the city. The red cross of St George was adopted as the arms of the city of London from the mid fourteenth century. On 17 April 1381 records show that the mayoralty seal of London was ordered to be changed. It would still feature St Paul and St Thomas à Becket, as had the earlier seal, but a shield was placed beneath their feet, featuring the cross of St George with a sword in the first quarter supported by lions. This instruction was given by the then Mayor of London, William Walworth.

The arms of London also feature two supporting, flanking dragons and the earliest record of these in relation to
the St George's cross dates from a manuscript of 1609
stored in the Guildhall library. However, it is worth noting
that dragons appear, flanking the city's patron St Paul, on
two embroidered seal bags dating from 1319. They are, of
course, more frequently associated with St George. Statues
of dragons can be found within the city of London and a
particularly striking example can be seen near the Temple
area on the embankment. Once it acted as a symbolic
guardian of the city boundaries.

Henry V is said to have invoked the aid of St George
during his military campaigns in France. Henry, who was
monarch of England from 1413 to 1422, laid siege to the
French town of Harfleur in 1415 and commanded that,
when it was taken, the flag of St George should be flown
over the city. Most famously, a vision of St George was said
to have been seen at the battle of Agincourt in 1415, an
English victory that is still remembered today as a great
national triumph against the odds. The English were outnumbered by the French and, during the battle, it was the
skill of English archers using longbows that proved deci-
sive. St George is also the patron saint of bowmen. William
Shakespeare immortalised the link between the king and
the saint in his play, *Henry V*. During Act III, Scene 1, Henry
addresses his troops with a rousing call to arms declaring
'Cry God for Harry! England! and St George!'.
(Interestingly, Shakespeare is thought to have been born on
St George's Day.)

Following the English victory at Agincourt the city of London mounted an extravagant celebration to honour the returning king. A ceremonial giant was created and installed at London Bridge, holding in its hands an axe as well as the keys to the city. As the king passed by he came to a wooden tower into which a decorated recess had been set. Inside the recess, about half way up the tower, 'there stood a most beautiful statue of St George in armour' (Maurice Keen, *English Social History in the Later Middle Ages*, p.114). A choir of boys was singing next to the statue of St George. Further into the city another tower was created which was decorated with arms of St Edmund, St Edward and the red cross of St George. The city was filled with pageantry and spectacle that even included a specially made wooden castle 'with a bridge from its gatehouse to the ground, over which a choir of maidens, dressed in virginal white, came out to greet the king, singing Welcome Henry the Fifth, King of England and of France' (Maurice Keen, *English Social History in the Later Middle Ages*, p115). Following the victory at Agincourt, St George's Day became of greater importance in England. Archbishop Chichele made the saint's feast day a major double feast or 'duplex maior' in 1415, which meant that it became as important in the annual English calendar as Christmas Day and Easter. Like these feast days, St George's Day was a major holiday and everyone was expected to desist from work and attend church in his honour.

During the middle ages the popularity of St George was not only restricted to the monarchy or to military celebrations. Many cities and towns formed Guilds of St George that could be joined for a fee. Entry to the guild carried certain responsibilities and duties but also gave individuals prestige and standing within the community. The guild would celebrate the feast day of its patron saint, collect alms and observe masses for members of the organisation who had died. The guild of St George was generally amongst the most powerful and prestigious of the guilds and very often wielded considerable political influence. The celebration of St George's Day was a major event in the yearly calendar and was marked by elaborate and often expensive parades and pageants. The 'Riding of the George' involved a procession of costumed individuals marching through the town, staging plays and dancing to the accompaniment of music. The figure of St George was paraded through the streets, together with a dragon, usually made of canvas and wickerwork, that one man could carry on his shoulders. The dragon was very often the most popular character within the parade. Civic celebrations at this time very often also featured a giant, such as was seen in the city of London's procession to mark the victory of the battle of Agincourt. The origins of the giant may have been pre-Christian, perhaps symbolising an ancient fertility or nature god. Many Celtic tales such as those collected in the *Mabinogion* featured giants who often possessed wondrous powers and skills. The presence of ceremonial giants in the civic pageants of the middle ages could stem from these older traditions. However, in a Christian context, it is thought that they are likely to have represented St

Christopher, patron saint of travellers and a giant in stature. Such processions were actually a continuation of older rituals and celebrations focused on the coming of spring that in time came to be organised and maintained by the medieval guilds.

A great deal of information has survived to the present day about the Norwich Guild of St George. The Norwich Guild was formed in 1389 and the primary purpose of the organisation was to attend mass on St George's Day. Records dating from 1408 show that the celebration of St George's Day took the form of a public procession in Norwich where a re-creation of the battle between George and the dragon was staged. Usually an actor, dressed in an expensive and rich costume, would assume the role of St George, although, in some years, a statue of the saint was conveyed through the town. In many ways, the celebrations of St George's Day were a mixture of religious devotions and displays of civic pride and status, and they would have been lively, jolly and noisy affairs with important or significant local dignitaries such as the mayor enjoying pride of place as the procession marched through the city. The dragon, which is recorded as being so designed that, by the use of gunpowder, sparks and smoke flew from his mouth, must have provided the townspeople with a great spectacle. The dragon came to be affectionately known as 'Snap' and, in addition to a mouth that could open and shut, had wings that could be operated and made to flap by the man inside the costume. The Snapdragon would threaten the onlookers by charging at them during the processional march. The route that the procession took began at the Cathedral and made its way through the city to a wood where the battle between St George and the dragon was performed by the costumed actors. The procession was led by a man carrying a gilded wooden sword that was said to have been given to the guild by Henry V, the king who had granted its charter. The handle of the sword was carved in the likeness of a dragon's head. Curiously, the actor who played the dragon received less money than the actor who played St George.

By 1532, another character, known as the Lady or 'the Margaret', had been included in the pageant to represent the princess whom St George saved in the *Golden Legend*. Her name probably derived from St Margaret who, as we saw in Chapter Two, was credited herself with killing a dragon. After the dramatisation of the conflict at the wood, the whole procession returned to the cathedral where a mass was celebrated. The dragon was symbolically left outside the cathedral and was placed on the 'dragon's stone'. After the service in the cathedral, the guild held a great feast. Early next day, a requiem mass was held to honour the guild's founder and the souls of deceased guildsmen.

Such events took place in many English cities and towns in the Middle Ages, including London, Leicester, York, Chichester, Reading, Chester and Coventry. As well as the 'Ridings', the story of St George was sometimes enacted in the form of a miracle play. Such a play is known to have been performed, for example, at Lydd in Kent during the fifteenth century.

In 1483, the publisher William Caxton printed his version of the *Golden Legend* and it proved hugely successful. Caxton included the story of George's battle with the dragon and this rapidly became the story most often associated with the saint. St George's popularity throughout English society was confirmed. His link with the English kings was maintained by Henry VI (1422–1461) and Henry VII (1485–1509). Henry VI inherited the devotion to the saint of his father, Henry V, and a special play, based on the life and legend of St George, was staged at his coronation in 1429. When Henry VII returned from exile in Brittany and landed on the Pembrokeshire coast to challenge Richard III for the throne of England, he is said to have knelt and prayed to St George for aid. Following his victory at the Battle of Bosworth in 1485, Henry VII presented a number of standards at St Paul's Cathedral, one of which was the flag of St George. He also had a painting commissioned for an altarpiece which depicted him and his family kneeling before a scene of St George fighting the dragon. (This relatively rare example of St George fighting a flying dragon was painted sometime in the first decade of the sixteenth century.) During the Wars of the Roses there is evidence that St George was popular with both sides and that, because he had come to be widely seen as the patron saint of the English kings, he was used in iconography to legitimise claims to the throne. The tomb of Henry VII at Westminster Abbey features several images of St George and the dragon and the king owned a relic of the saint, allegedly a piece of his leg bone.

However, it was during the reign of Henry VIII that St George was most firmly and definitively established as patron saint of England. The arms of St George became the flag of England and Henry VIII issued coins that bore images of George and the dragon. Henry, who ruled from 1509 to 1547, also used images of the saint on his own suits of armour and on one of his crowns. He maintained the Order of the Garter, with its clear links to the saint, and appears to have had a special veneration or admiration for St George. This is most clearly demonstrated by the fact that, when Henry abolished nearly all religious holidays in 1536, he excepted only a very few. One of these few was the feast of St George. (The others that were to be maintained were the feasts of the Apostles and the Virgin Mary.) In 1547 an Act of Parliament was passed that banned the guilds and their processions. However, many of the guilds were amended or re-organised and survived, although the nature of the processions changed. In 1552 the Bishop of London banned St George's Day. This ban seems to have been largely ignored but, during this period, the traditional 'ridings' on St George's Day moved away from a purely religious devotion to the saint and became more secular events, celebrating civic pride and power. In some instances, George himself was left out of the parade although the dragon was retained. In Norwich, the Snapdragon was paraded until 1732 when the guild of St George was dissolved. The status of St George at all levels of society, as patron saint of farmers, soldiers, archers and armourers and as a saint associated with healing, meant that the iconoclasm of the Reformation did not undermine his popularity greatly, although it can be said to have contributed to a move to a more secular identity for the saint. The adoption of St George by the English is taken a step further in Richard Johnson's work of 1597, *The Most Famous History of the Seven Champions of Christendom*, in which it is claimed that he was born in Coventry. Johnson tells the story of George and the dragon but, in his version, the saint actually marries the Princess who is a daughter of the sultan of Egypt called Sabra. They have three children and the story, reflecting the values of the period, emphasises the importance of the family. No longer a symbol of chastity, George is presented here as a masculine patriarch and Johnson's narrative ignores the circumstances of his martyrdom.

The influence of St George on the shaping of English culture in the middle ages was dramatic and profound but it is important to recognise also the power of his patronage beyond these shores. Many may be surprised to discover that St George is also the patron saint of Ethiopia. The emperors of Ethiopia led their soldiers into battle under the banner of St George which depicts him defeating the dragon. His image can be found in churches throughout Ethiopia and perhaps one of the most unusual buildings dedicated in his name can be found there. 'Bet Giorgis' or the 'House of St George' is believed to have been created by King Lalibela who ruled Ethiopia from 1167 to 1207. It is the largest and most important of twelve churches that form two separate groups close to the river Jordan.

Astonishingly, each church is carved from a single piece of stone and they are often referred to as monolithic or rock churches.

The churches are thought to have been created within a one-hundred-year period around 1200. According to legend, King Lalibela was visited by St George when the churches had almost been completed. Riding a white horse and dressed in armour, St George demanded to know why the king had not dedicated a church in his honour. King Lalibela replied that he would make the most important and impressive church of the twelve for St George. St George oversaw the construction of the church himself. Bet Giorgis is nearly twelve meters tall and takes the form of a cube which has then been cut into the shape of a cross. Set below ground level and surrounded by an excavated pit, the church is reached through an entrance tunnel. The flat cruciform roof features three Greek crosses of diminishing size, set one within another. Architecturally, it merges early Christian Mediterranean styles with the traditions of the Axumite Empire to create a singular Ethiopian vision. The churches are still in use today and are hugely significant to the people of Ethiopia. Their religious denomination is Ethiopian Orthodox, which in turn is part of the Alexandria-based Coptic Christian Church.

Europeans, who did not think it possible that Ethiopians could have created such remarkable buildings, started false rumours that the Knights Templar built the churches during the thirteenth century. The concept of a church hewn from a single block of stone is not, however, unique to Ethiopia. Interestingly, Goreme in Cappadocia, the region in Turkey with which St George is very often associated, has a number of churches carved from local rock formations. At Yilanli church in Goreme there is a fresco of St George with St Theodore, another well-known soldier saint. They are both depicted on horseback, battling with a gigantic snake that St George is spearing with his lance. The churches range in date from the ninth to the eleventh centuries AD. Other examples of monolithic churches include the church of St Jean in Aubeterre-sur-Dronne and Saint-Romain abbey in Beaucaire, both in France. Arguably, the monolithic churches can be seen to represent a fusing of pre-Christian and Christian practices where the worship of stones gives way to a church created from a single stone.

Hero of the Empire

Despite the waxing and waning of St George's popularity during the Reformation, the power of his myth took on new potency during the Counter Reformation. As Western explorers opened up new territories in countries such as India and the Americas, missionaries would carry his legend beyond the confines of Europe. St George was the champion of the church and, as a result, his name can now be found in many countries around the globe. The story of St George, both as martyr and dragon-slayer, inspired the Protestant author John Bunyan in the writing of his most famous work, *Pilgrim's Progress*, published in two parts in 1679 and 1684. The central character of this allegorical work is called Christian and he engages in a fight with the terrible Apollyon who is a dragon-like figure. The combat takes the form of argument and ends with Christian striking Apollyon with his sword, causing him to disappear. The story of St George and the dragon continued to inspire and shape societies and cultures beyond the height of its fame in the middle ages.

The church of St George's-in-the-East in Wapping, London was designed by the architect Nicholas

Hawksmoor and built between 1714 and 1729, and was named at least in part in honour of the king. Hawksmoor also designed St George's church in Bloomsbury that was built between 1716 and 1731. They were both commissioned as a result of the 'Fifty New Churches Act' of 1711. Hawksmoor's design for St George's in Bloomsbury was influenced by a description by the Latin author Pliny of the ancient Mausoleum at Halicarnassus. The pyramidal steeple is topped by a statue of King George I in classical dress, wearing a toga. (It is apparently the only surviving statue of the king in Britain.) His appearance strongly recalls Eastern images of St George as a Roman soldier and it seems likely that the king is being equated with the saint. The church was used by Dickens as the setting for a christening in *Sketches by Boz* (1837). In recent years the writer Iain Sinclair has argued that the churches of Nicholas Hawksmoor form a strange mystical grid or pattern. Interestingly, Emperor Haile Selassie of Ethiopia took part in a requiem for the dead of the Abyssinian war in 1937 at St George's, Bloomsbury (St George, as we have seen, is patron saint of Ethiopia).

As we saw in Chapter One, the historian Edward Gibbon questioned the true identity of St George in his multi-volume work *The History of the Decline and Fall of the Roman Empire*, published between 1776 and 1788. He suggested that St George the patron saint of England could be identified with another George of Cappadocia. This George of Cappadocia had been an Archbishop of Alexandria who was known to be sympathetic to the Arian heresy. This heresy argued that Jesus Christ had not been divine but simply a man. The archbishop died in 362 AD at the hands of an angry mob. Gibbon's theory had many critics although it is, of course, possible that elements of the story of the heretical archbishop may have found their way into the story of George the Martyr. Perhaps the most evidence that there had been a 'real' St George emerged with the discovery, during the nineteenth century, of the early churches in Syria dedicated to him. Yet, while scholars continued to argue about the identity of St George, the influence of his legend remained powerful.

Continuing the link between English royalty and St George, the Prince Regent, who was to become George IV, founded the Most Distinguished Order of St Michael and St George in 1818. Its purpose was to recognise outstanding service in the diplomatic service. Initially, this honour was only extended to the citizens of the Ionian Islands and Malta and British people who had served in the diplomatic service there. The Palace of St Michael and St George on the Ionian island of Corfu dates from this period of the British protectorate and was built between 1819 and 1824 under the first High Commissioner, Sir Thomas Maitland. The British were also responsible for building the Church of St George that served the garrison in the Old Fortress of Corfu Town. Both buildings are built in the neo-classical style that derived from Greek architecture of antiquity. William IV re-structured the order into three different classes of award, comprising of Knight Grand Cross (GCMG), Knight Commander (KCMG) and Companion

(CMG). In 1879 the honour was extended to any individual who had served in the Commonwealth countries. Today, the order, which originally applied only to men, recognises women with the alternative category of 'Dame'. The medals issued by the order feature St George and the Dragon on one side and, on the reverse, St Michael defeating the devil. The medal also carries the legend '*auspicium melioris aevi*' which translates as 'augury of a better age'. St Paul's Cathedral is the Chapel of the Order.

St George was to prove a source of inspiration for the Pre-Raphaelites who shared a fascination with medieval culture and romantic chivalry. William Morris created a stained glass window with his fellow Pre-Raphaelite Dante Gabriel Rossetti called *The Wedding of St George and the Princess*. Their version of the story of St George draws not on the earlier lives of the saint, in which he does not marry the princess, but on Richard Johnson's *The Most Famous History of the Seven Champions of Christendom* of 1597. In the stained glass window St George views the severed head of the dragon lying on a platter with a sword. St George is holding the hand of the princess who, unsurprisingly, conforms to the wavy, auburn-haired image of so many Pre-Raphaelite heroines. St George could himself be easily mistaken for a self-portrait by one of the 'brotherhood'. (Coincidentally, upon his death in 1896, Morris was buried in the graveyard of St George's church, Kelmscott, near Oxford.) Edward Burne-Jones, another member of the movement, produced a painting entitled *St George and the Dragon* in 1868, portraying the saint as a beautiful youth, looking more like a romantic poet than the sturdy champion of the English army. The world famous Liberty's store in London, which originally opened in 1875 and included many of the artists of the pre-Raphaelite movement in its clientele, sold goods that drew their inspiration from a romanticised version of the middle ages. Its striking mock Tudor frontage has a clock with moving figures at its far right-hand side. When the clock tolls the hour, a moving figurine of St George, mounted on a white charger, strikes a green dragon with his lance in a perpetual struggle fought above the heads of London shoppers. The clock provides an interesting example of the way in which St George took on an increasingly secular identity in English society. His origins as a martyr become obscured and his image appears on any number of British goods in a context where St George indicates nothing more than a standard of excellence and craftsmanship with which manufacturers are keen to identify themselves.

The artist and critic John Ruskin founded the Guild of St George in 1871, an organisation that was intended to promote patriotism and also to fight the worse extremes of industrialised society. The aim of the guild was to work for decent treatment and housing for workers and to develop agricultural skills in educational centres. It is striking that Ruskin, who was motivated by ideals of fairness and decency and a genuine desire to improve the lives of ordinary people, should choose St George as the patron of his Guild. St George, by this time, had come to represent not only the epitome of the chivalrous, valiant knight who righted wrongs but was also the exemplary model of the English concept of 'fair play'. Whether real or imagined, this ideal had become inextricably linked with the figure of St George.

The reputation of St George as the epitome of the chivalrous knight led to his being adopted as the patron saint of the Boy Scout movement in 1908. Lieutenant-General Robert Baden-Powell, a national hero at the time, founded the movement. Baden-Powell had joined the 13th Hussars in India in 1876 and, by 1897, commanded the 5th Dragoon Guards. Whilst serving in South Africa and organising a group of specialist 'frontiersmen' who were intended to aid the regular British army, Baden-Powell became trapped in the town of Mafeking. In the ensuing siege, a large Boer army surrounded the British garrison who were heavily outnumbered. Nonetheless they withstood the siege for 217 days before the arrival of a British relief force. The Siege of Mafeking made Baden-Powell a celebrity and he was to draw on the skills and experiences he had gained in the military in founding the Boy Scouts. He wrote *Scouting for Boys* in 1908, which became hugely successful, and paved the way for the launch of the movement. Baden-Powell believed that English boys should aspire to chivalrous behaviour, bravery and self-discipline and devised activities and games that would promote such qualities. Aimed at boys aged between 11 and 15, the movement rapidly spread from England to other countries, including America, South Africa and Australia. Today the Boy Scout Movement can be found in over 100 countries world-wide. On St George's Day scouts remember their Scout Promise and the Scout Law, parades take place all over Britain and special services are held in local churches. In *Scouting for Boys*, Baden-Powell made the claim that King Arthur's Knights of the Round Table had chosen St George as their patron because 'he was the only one of all the saints who was a horseman. He is the patron saint of cavalry, from which the word chivalry is derived'. Other works, such as *The Life of St George, the Patron Soldier-Saint of England* by Alice Brewster (1907), appeared at this time, which further attempted to link King Arthur and his knights with St George. The imagery of the Boy Scout movement often featured St George and the dragon, usually alongside the Union Jack and Scout mottoes such as 'Be Prepared'. The cover of Baden-Powell's *Young Knights of the Empire*, published in 1916, features an illustration which shows a boy in armour, holding a shield with the fleur-de-lis emblem of the scouts and a spear. The red-cross banner of St George is flying from the spear and the boy is looking through the bars of a cage at a trapped dragon. In this instance the dragon in question has not merely been defeated but appears positively depressed, as a wisp of smoke rises from its nostrils. Upon the bars of the cage appear the legends 'Honour God and the King', 'Obey the law of the scouts', and 'Do a good turn to somebody every day'.

Baden-Powell was not the only writer to create a link between St George and King Arthur. In 1929, an anonymous author published a work entitled *St George at Glastonbury*. In this account of the life of the saint, George is born in Cornwall and travels to Coventry with his mother as a child. Later, St George sets out for Glastonbury in order to heal his sick mother. His prayers are answered and he is made a knight and handed the legendary sword, Excalibur. The writer claims that it is the same sword that would be later carried by king Arthur and later still Richard the Lionheart. This story weaves together a number of different traditions, including Richard Johnson's claim from *The Most Famous History of the Seven Champions of Christendom* that St George was born in Coventry. Interestingly, the book also makes the claim that St George the Dragon slayer and St George the Christian martyr are in fact two different people. In *St George at Glastonbury*, it would seem that the legend had finally come to obscure the man completely.

The location of St George within contexts that were often nationalistic, racist and imperialistic is exemplified by his appearance in the children's play *Where the Rainbow Ends*, first performed in 1911. Written by Mrs Clifford Mills, it was hugely successful from the first and remained so for decades. It was performed annually and has been compared to J. M. Barrie's *Peter Pan* in terms of its popularity, being performed regularly at Christmas. The story concerns two children, Crispian and his sister Rosamund, who have lost their parents. They are forced to live with an unpleasant Uncle and Aunt who are planning to sell the house they have been bequeathed to a German-Jewish man called Schnapps. The children remember a book called the 'Rainbow Book' that gives directions to the

'Land Where All Lost Loved Ones Are Found'. The children summon a genie that grants them each two wishes. Crispian wishes for the help of his best friend 'Blunders' who appears with his sister Betty. Rosamund makes the wish that St George should appear to help them in their distress. When he appears he is a disappointing and sad figure, an old man without a sword, who has been neglected by the English. However, when Rosamund asks for his help as a 'damsel in distress', his appearance immediately changes and he becomes a young hero in shining armour with blonde hair and blue eyes. They escape on 'Faith's magic carpet' and travel to the safety of the kingdom of St George.

Later, the children are captured by the Dragon King. He plans to have them thrown from the battlements of his castle for choosing St George as their patron. But the plan is foiled when Crispian and his best friend 'Blunders' make a St George's flag and substitute it for the banner of the dragon. Immediately, St George appears and rescues them, killing the Dragon King. St George re-unites the children with their parents and they take him back to England 'to live henceforth and forever in the hearts of the children of his race'. St George's final words at the end of the play are: 'Rise, Youth of England, let your voices ring/For God, for Britain, and for Britain's King'.

Such sentiments and some of the disturbingly racist imagery of the play have contributed to the negative associations many make today between the figure of St George and discredited notions of national identity and patriotism.

At the Battle of Mons in 1914, during the First World War, there were numerous reports from British troops that visions of St George had been seen over the battlefield. The British army had been forced into a difficult and dangerous retreat at Mons. Despite much greater German numbers, however, they successfully withdrew and held the line and it was claimed that St George, who had appeared leading a ghostly army, had aided them. A writer called Arthur Machen produced a short story called 'The Bowmen' for the *London Evening News* in the same year, based on these reports. The story was later printed in book form and Machen went on to argue that it was his story that had sparked the reports in the first place. However, his theory was attacked by many people, including an author called Harold Begbie who wrote a riposte to Machen entitled *On the Side of the Angels: an Answer to the 'Bowmen'*.

In his book, Begbie quoted eye-witness accounts of the Battle of Mons by soldiers that had been reported before the publication of 'The Bowmen'. 'Begbie's informants claimed to have seen a wide range of visions, including knights, bowmen, saints, glowing angels, mysterious clouds (hiding them from the enemy) and phantom armies' (Jon Michell and Bob Rickard, *Unexplained Phenomena*, p.219). This was further supported by a Lieutenant Colonel who contacted Arthur Machen to say that, together with his entire brigade, he had witnessed strange, spectral cavalry riding with them at Mons. There were even reports that dead German soldiers had been found with wounds caused by arrows. St George was also said to have been present at

Vity-le-Francois during the First World War, leading the British army into battle and riding on a white horse. As with the visions of St George reported during the crusades and at Agincourt (echoed in the appearances at Mons), such sightings give an indication, at the very least, of the esteem in which the saint has been held by English soldiers for centuries.

Following the First World War, the artist Adrian Jones created the Cavalry Memorial in Serpentine Road in London's Hyde Park, which shows St George defeating the dragon. A piece of broken lance protrudes from the dragon's neck and St George is triumphantly holding his sword aloft in the moment of victory. Jones had been a veterinary surgeon within the cavalry and the choice of St George for the monument is apt, given his status as patron saint of soldiers, horsemen and horses. A similar memorial to the dead of both wars can be found in front of St John's Wood church in London, close to Lord's cricket ground. A bronze sculpture by C L Hartwell depicts St George seated on a rearing charger and dressed in medieval armour, having vanquished the dragon. It serves as a 'grateful tribute to the men and women of Saint-Mary-Le-Bone' and illustrates the role of St George as 'champion of the British Empire'. Indeed, Adrian Jones's Hyde Park memorial is dedicated to the Cavalry of the Empire and depicts not only English but Indian soldiers in a sequence of reliefs around its base. A second cast of Hartwell's sculpture was made and now stands in the city of Newcastle, as a monument to the soldiers of that city who died during the two world wars. Both sculptures portray the saint as a western knight and there is no hint of his Eastern origins as an early Christian martyr. In these monuments, St George has become an icon of 'Englishness', as English as the game of cricket played at Lord's, close by Hartwell's sculpture.

Another interesting identification of St George with British soldiers in the First World War can be found at St James's church in Marylebone, London. In a side chapel dedicated to the British dead of the armed forces there is a series of three stained glass windows. They feature St George who symbolises the army, St Michael for the air force and the Virgin Mary representing the navy. St George is depicted wearing the uniform of an infantryman but is instantly identifiable by the white tabard with a red cross sign that he is wearing over it. However, even in this modern imagining of St George, he is standing over a defeated green dragon. St Michael is portrayed with a defeated red dragon at his feet. In a lower section of the window featuring St George there is an inset of a horse-drawn carriage from the First World War and, in the window of St Michael, there is an inset of an RAF biplane. Appropriately enough St James's stands on George Street, close to a pub called the 'Angel in the Fields'.

During the Second World War, the actor Sir Laurence Olivier directed and starred in a film version of Shakespeare's *Henry V*. Intended to be a rousing, morale-boosting work that would act as a call to arms, it was financed in part by the British government. Released in 1944, its patriotic theme of an English victory in France against the odds mirrored, in many ways, the circumstances of the war. As the American critic James Agee commented in his review of the film for *Time* on 8 April 1946, 'The man who made this movie made it midway in England's most terrible war, within the shadows of Dunkirk. In appearance and in most of what they say, the three soldiers with whom Henry talks on the eve of Agincourt might just as well be soldiers of World War II'. This of course gave an extraordinary resonance to the often-quoted speech that Henry gives to his troops, 'I see you stand like greyhounds in the slips, straining upon the start. The game's afoot; follow your spirit; and upon this charge, Cry God for Harry! England! And Saint George!' The small craft and little boats that had helped to rescue the British Army at Dunkirk in 1940 were afterwards granted the right to fly the 'Dunkirk Jack', the banner of St George, in recognition of their bravery during the evacuation and for service to their country.

In 1940, King George VI created the George Cross in response to the bravery of the British people in enduring the bombing raids of the blitz. The George Cross was intended to recognise 'acts of the greatest heroism or of the most conspicuous courage in circumstances of extreme danger'. Of similar status to the Victoria Cross, it is usually awarded to civilians. The award can also be made posthumously. The George Cross is made of silver and, on one side, is an image of St George slaying the dragon and an inscription that reads 'For Gallantry'. The reverse side bears the name of the individual to whom the award has been given with the date of its issue. George VI also created the George Medal that recognises similar acts of bravery and courage but of a lesser degree. This medal also features St George and the dragon and an image of the current monarch on the reverse. Famously, the people of the island of Malta were awarded the George Cross in 1942 for their outstanding bravery and resistance during the Second World War.

St George is the patron saint of Gozo the second largest island in the Maltese archipelago. The Basilica of St George in the island capital of Victoria was built in 1678 and designed by the architect Vittorio Cassar. The capital was known as Rabat, meaning simply 'the town', until 1897 when the British Governor altered its name to celebrate the Diamond Jubilee of Queen Victoria. The Gozitan artist Paola Azzopardi carved a wooden statue of St George from a single tree for the Basilica. Gozitans celebrate the saint on the third Sunday in July when the skyline of the town is crowded with the red-cross banners of St George. During the day, horses and chariots are raced along the main street of the town and a lavish (and dangerous!) firework display is held at night. The Pjazza San Gorg is filled with people and they celebrate the festival of the saint with gusto. Just as the festivals of medieval England were often accompanied by wild and drunken behaviour, the celebration on Gozo has in some years necessitated mounted Maltese police being ferried over to control the revellers.

St George is also patron saint of the city of Moscow and he is an important and popular saint throughout Russia. The flag of Moscow, which dates back to the middle ages, still features an image of the saint slaying the dragon today. The seal of Vasiliy Dmitriyevich, prince of Moscow, dates from 1390 and shows a horseman carrying a spear. The image is known as 'St George the victory bearer', a popular epithet for the saint. The dragon was added during the reign of Ivan III, Duke of Moscow, who reigned from 1462 to 1505. Because of his presence in the arms of Moscow, St George is also featured on the Coat of Arms of the Russian Federation, together with the larger symbol of the double-headed eagle that was the symbol of the Byzantine Empire. (The two heads denote the role of the Byzantine Empire, extending both East and West.) Following the Communist revolution, the coat of arms of the Old Russian Empire was abandoned but it was re-adopted after the fall of the Soviet Union. During the Second World War, Soviet Army General Georgiy Zhukov was photographed symbolically riding a white horse over a heap of Nazi regalia in Red Square, Moscow. This gesture, carried out in 1944, affirmed the long link between the people of Moscow and their patron saint.

St George, usually depicted on horseback trampling down the dragon, can also be found on numerous war memorials in Russia. One anti-fascist Russian propaganda poster of World War II depicts a Russian soldier bayoneting a huge snake that has contorted its body into the shape of a swastika, another echo of the tradition of 'dragon slaying' of which St George is such a notable part. It is common in Russia to celebrate not only birthdays but 'name days'.

People are very often named after saints and the celebrations usually involve a remembrance of the story of the saint after which they have been named. Russian variations on the name George include Yuri and Georgi.

Saint George as Icon

Following the disillusionment of the First World War and the trauma of the Second World War, St George increasingly seemed to represent a relic from another era in England. His popularity as a symbol of the British Empire made him an uncomfortable icon for many people during the major post-war changes in attitudes to imperialism and colonialism. In more recent years, there has been an increasing tendency for St George to be appropriated and manipulated by far right groups in England with a racist or jingoistic agenda. An example of this trend towards using the saint as the representative of an inward-looking and aggressive form of nationalism is 'The League of St George', founded in 1975. This organisation supports the idea of 'England for the English' and, in arguing that England belongs to those who have an ancestral right to call themselves English, members propound the importance of maintaining a racially pure national identity. The belief that countries belong to the 'folk' and that 'foreign' individuals need to be expelled has, of course, disturbing parallels with the fascist ideology of Nazism. The implication of St George in such xenophobic and racist beliefs indicates the extent to which the true nature of his identity has been forgotten, suppressed or distorted. It seems supremely ironic that an early Christian martyr, of Palestinian or Turkish descent, who fought for his religious freedom should become an emblem of English extremism. At times, St George has come to be viewed as a symbol of 'Englishness' in the same way that other cartoon figures, such as Britannia and John Bull, are. Godfrey Smith, writing in 1984 about the decline of the relationship between the English and their patron saint, commented that St George '(has) become something of an embarrassment to the English, most of whom do not even know what their national flag, the Cross of St George, looks like' (Godfrey Smith, *The English Companion*, p.223). More recently, the television presenter and journalist Jeremy Paxman dismissed St George as 'a vague, workaday saint of little spiritual or theological importance' (Jeremy Paxman, *The English*). The Roman Catholic Church officially downgraded the feast day of St George to an optional local festival in 1969. The importance of the saint in the United Kingdom was acknowledged by the Catholic Church by its decision to make St George's Day a major feast in England and Wales. In 1997 the General Synod of the Church of England restored 23 April to the level of a major religious holiday in the Anglican calendar.

St George may often have been appropriated by the far right in England but, in complete contrast, he has also served in recent years as a powerful emblem of Rastafarianism. On the cover of Bob Marley's 1983 album

Confrontation, released two years after the singer's death, Marley is shown adopting the role of St George, riding on a white horse and slaying a dragon. As we saw in Chapter Six, St George is the patron saint of Ethiopia, the spiritual centre of Rastafarianism. The image, designed by the artist Neville Garrick, shows Marley using a traditional Ethiopian thong stirrup – an intended reference to the cancer which claimed his life and which started in his toe as a result of an injury sustained playing football. Like St George, Bob Marley is a hero to many and it is interesting to find these two icons equated in this way. In his original artwork for the album, Garrick depicted the dragon wearing a mitre and this was intended to represent the papacy. The reference to the papacy as the satanic dragon was linked to revelations in 1981 that members of the then Italian government had been involved in a secret Masonic order called P2 who had links to the Vatican, the Mafia and the CIA. Some Rastafarians considered that Freemasons were pagans who believed that Solomon had gained occult power from Hiram Abiff, the architect who built the Temple of Jerusalem. Some claimed that Abiff had turned his back on God and worshipped the deity Baal. As punishment God had destroyed that Temple in the same way that the tower of Babel, also constructed by Masons, had been ruined. Many Rastas also believed that the papacy had supported Mussolini's invasion of Ethiopia in the 1930s. In the event Chris Blackwell, the head of Marley's record company Island Records, fearful of offending Catholics world-wide, refused to allow the image to be used. The final image can be read in a number of ways – both as a condemnation of the alleged corruption of the Roman Catholic church, as Garrick originally intended it, or, more generally, as good defeating evil with Marley cast in the role of righteous victor, the first 'third world superstar' and champion of Rastafarianism. The inner sleeve artwork shows St George leading the Ethiopians in a victorious battle against Italian forces.

St George may have been featured in unpleasantly nationalistic contexts in England in recent years but this does not seem to have affected the popularity of the flag of St George. The red cross banner seems to have developed a genuinely multi-cultural appeal and appears regularly in contemporary English society on everything from T-shirts and baseball hats to car stickers, key-rings and, of course, flags. Its most common association is with sport and it is particularly identified with football. Where many feel uncomfortable with displaying the Union flag, the Union Jack, because of its appropriation by far right groups, the same stigma does not seem to apply to the flag of St George. The appearance of the red-cross banner at sporting and cultural events also reflects the growing distinction between a 'British' and an 'English' identity as the process of devolution in the United Kingdom unfolds. During the Euro 96 football tournament held in England a St George and the dragon pageant was staged at Wembley.

Curious parallels can be drawn between St George and today's icon David Beckham, the captain of the England football team. Like George, Beckham has served as a national hero for England and a multi-cultural icon with a far broader appeal in many countries. In the same way that St George is often represented in a way that reflects the nationality of the country that is revering him (in Greek icons, for example, he has a Mediterranean appearance), Beckham appears at times to have a multi-racial appeal. Indeed, a tabloid obsession with Beckham's corn row hair style and interest in popular black street fashion reflects St George's own strangely polymorphous identity.

Beckham, like St George, has also served as sex symbol and fertility figure and, like pre-Raphaelite representations of the saint, he has been viewed as the archetypal 'beautiful young man'. Beckham is also a gay icon and was photographed topless for the magazine *Attitude* striking a crucifixion pose in front a giant St George's red cross. Samantha Riches has identified variants of the cult of St George in the Coptic Churches of North East Africa in which the saint is 'identified as a bridegroom of Christ', (Samantha Riches, *St George, Hero, Martyr and Myth*, p.214). There appears to be a tradition of a platonic union between the two but Riches suggests that St George himself has also served as a gay icon. Interestingly, in a recent television documentary about Windsor Castle, the deacon of the Chapel of St George rejected an image of the saint that was to appear on the re-branded logo of its shop on the grounds that it was 'too effeminate'. The image had been taken from a medieval tapestry and was passed over in favour of a more unequivocally masculine image of St George from the Victorian era. Just as people in the past interpreted and re-interpreted St George in varying and, sometimes, conflicting ways, so the process continues today.

Such observations might, at first, seem absurd but Beckham's images can be compared with representations of other sporting heroes. In 1968, the boxer Muhammad Ali appeared in a photograph published in the magazine *Esquire* in a pose based on the painting 'The Martyrdom of St Sebastian' by Andrea del Castagno. Photographer Carl Fischer called his image 'The Passion of Muhammad Ali' and it shows Ali dressed in his white boxing shorts and shoes. He is standing with his hands tied behind his back and he is pierced with arrows. The picture alludes to Ali's treatment by the American government and the white establishment and, on publication, it proved both popular and controversial. As a Muslim, Ali has strong religious beliefs himself, but, as a sports personality, he is a secular hero. The fusing of 'sacred' imagery and secular culture in images like Fischer's raises questions about the nature of celebrity and its role in modern society. Richard Howells of the University of Leeds has argued that 'The Passion of Muhammad Ali' continues the tradition of the medieval relic. Perhaps we should reflect upon our often-casual use of the term 'icon' and what exactly it denotes to people today. The writer Nicholas Mann has commented that, 'Today, as in the past, we select champions to represent us', (Nicholas Mann, *Reclaiming the Gods*, p.105). Beckham and Ali are such champions and, like St George, they represent the deep-seated, ancient need for heroes within human societies.

One interesting example of the way in which St George's identity has been largely transformed in England, from that of an early Christian martyr into a secular folk figure, is the naming of a shopping centre in his honour in Harrow, Middlesex. The St George's shopping centre enshrines the legend of his conflict with the dragon in its scaly-tailed logo and the sequence of narrative reliefs high above the heads of the public on its walls. Of course, the shops provide the focus of the centre and yet, oddly, the architect appears to have designed the building, with its cruciform ground plan, in the style of a church. It is often argued that, as Western society has grown increasingly secular, shopping and materialism have emerged as substitutes for religion and it is interesting to see how England's patron saint has become part of this cultural change.

The link between the English royal family and St George has remained strong up to the present day. The Order of the Garter, of which he is patron, is still in existence and the royal family has one of its homes at Windsor today. St George's Chapel at Windsor has been at the centre of several major royal events in recent years, including the burial of the Queen Mother (many thousands subsequently visited her tomb) and the marriage between Prince Charles and Camilla Parker-Bowles. Perhaps, just as the monarchs of the past bolstered their right to rule through association with St George, so recent royals have looked to the saint to aid them in difficult times.

The general decline in the popularity of St George's Day is in marked contrast to the increased tendency of the

Welsh, Scottish and Irish to celebrate the feast days of their patron saints. St Patrick's Day, in particular, has become an opportunity for widespread and exuberant festivities and a happy, if sometimes superficial, celebration of Irish culture. In the recent past, attempts have been made to re-invigorate interest in the feast day of St George by groups such as the 'St George's Day Association' but they have been met, largely, with indifference. However, as England is increasingly defined as a country which has an identity informed by, but separate from, its near neighbours, the question of whether greater efforts should be made to celebrate St George's Day seems to be increasing in importance. On 23 April 2005, *The Sun* reported that the cricketer Ian Botham had taken a petition to 10 Downing Street calling for St George's Day to be made a national holiday. It was said to have been signed by half a million people who supported the idea. Botham was quoted as saying: 'Why shouldn't it be a national holiday? Our heritage is being eroded. Large numbers of people don't know anything about St George and yet we see the flag raised at cricket and football grounds. My message is people should be proud to be English, supporting the patron saint and English products.' The same issue of the newspaper reported a story about the Royal Navy banning 12 warships from flying the St George's flag. The ban was allegedly imposed at the Devonport Naval base in Plymouth because Naval authorities did not want to upset a visiting Turkish warship, the *Orucreis*. Perhaps predictably, *The Sun* and *The Daily Mail* described it as 'political correctness gone mad' and pointed out that St George may well have been Turkish, that he is the patron saint of Istanbul and that St George's Day is also Turkish National Sovereignty Day as well. Clearly, some people continue to think that St George is uncomfortably linked to England's imperial past and the spectre of colonialism.

The Pocket Book of Patriotism by George Courtauld has been a major and unexpected publishing success recently. It is a book that shows, according to its author, that there is 'an enormous and uplifting groundswell of people who are intensely proud of being English'. Interestingly, although St George makes an appearance on the cover of the book, fighting the dragon, there is very little mention of the saint within its pages. Courtauld refers to the famous battle cry of Shakespeare's play *Henry V* but omits it from his pages. The image of St George is outlined in gold and is instantly recognisable but the face of the saint is not depicted. The cover seems a strangely appropriate portrayal of a national saint whose complex identity seems now obscured for the nation that adopted him. The book contains a page that depicts the national flags of England, Scotland and Wales, lists the imperial territories of the British Empire in 1920 and provides full transcriptions of 'Rule Britannia' and 'Jerusalem'. The overall design of the book was intended to 'look like a cross between the old British passport and an old school text book called Kennedy's Latin Primer'. Clearly, there is a widespread interest in English history and achievements but, for many people, this is often accompanied by confusion over what those 'achievements' might be and whether or not they should be celebrated.

The renewed interest in celebrating St George's Day has also led to a revival of other English folk traditions, such as Morris dancing and Mummer's Plays. Interestingly, both of these folk practices have links with St George, although the evidence for the presence of the saint in Morris dancing is admittedly sketchy. Although it is often thought to be peculiarly English, Morris dancing is a kind of folk dance that is found in other cultures as well. Documents from the middle ages record such dances in England and references to it occur in other European countries such as Spain and France. However, it is thought to have derived from much earlier traditional dances that were never recorded. In England, they were danced during springtime Whitsun celebrations often known as 'Ales'. As noted in Chapter Six, such festivities were important events in the yearly calendar and offered an opportunity for revelry and enjoyment in communities across England. Predictably, the puritan movement strongly disapproved of 'Ales' and banned them, although Charles II later restored them. There are currently three main styles of Morris dancing, each defined by its regional origins. They are the Border Morris, the North West Morris and the Cotswold Morris dances. It is known that a dragon sometimes appeared in the dances and some believe that St George would have ridden upon it. The argument is supported by the fact that such dances often included other popular folk figures such as Robin Hood and Maid Marion. More generalised figures, such as hobby-horses and clowns, also took part. Such figures rose and fell in their interest to their audiences and, as Ronald Hutton observed, 'by the mid 1520s, in fact, the popularity of the Robin Hood theme was waning ...' (Ronald Hutton, *The Rise and Fall of Merry England*, p.67). It may be that St George suffered a similar fate.

However, the saint is more unequivocally linked to the performance of mummers' plays in which he is a key character. Mummers' plays are thought to have early origins, although most only date from the 1800s. Once again, this form of folk performance is found, in various styles, throughout Europe and deal with what are, essentially, universal themes and concepts. There is considerable debate over the origin of the term 'mummer'. Some suggest it derives from an old English word 'mum' that means silent and that the plays may originally have been performed silently as pantomimes. Others have conjectured it is linked to the Greek term for mask, 'mommo'. They were often performed on 'Plough Monday' or other important spring dates but are best known for being staged in mid-winter. The chief characters are the hero, known as St George or King George, and the villain, usually known as the Turkish or Persian knight. The central event in the play is a fight between the two. The other key character in the play is the Doctor who has the power to restore one or other of the characters to life.

In some of the plays St George himself is killed but magically restored by the doctor, an act which reflects the legend of his resurrections in the story of his martyrdom. The central themes of the mummers' plays are the battle between good and evil and the idea of resurrection or revival. The times of year in which they are performed are important. In springtime the desire for new growth or re-birth is strong and, in the darkest part of winter, the concern is that nature and fertility will be renewed. Symbolically, St George defeats the villain, representing winter, so that spring can come once again. As noted in earlier chapters, St George has close links to fertility and is the patron saint of farmers. The name George in Greek means 'farmer' and derives from 'geo' or earth. The name George denotes someone who works with the land or 'urges' the soil.

Although there is considerable regional variation amongst mumming plays, St George usually gives a victory speech that provides a sense of the style of the performance and alludes to Richard Johnson's version of the legend of St George in *The Most Famous History of the Seven Champions of Christendom*. In a mumming play performed in Burford, Oxfordshire, in which St George fights the dragon and not a human foe, the saint is first defeated by the dragon but revived by the doctor. He then fights the dragon a second time and defeats it and the doctor does not perform his feat of resurrection. The victory speech from the Burford play is:

"Here am I, St George, that worthy champion bold,
And with my sword and spear I won three crowns of gold.
I fought the fiery dragon and brought him to the slaughter,
And by that I won fair Sabra, the King of Egypt's daughter."
(Ralph Whitlock, *Here Be Dragons*, p.25)

In recent years, both Morris dancing and mummers' plays have been performed on St George's Day.

One commentator who has spoken of the need to reclaim the saint in England from his associations with bigotry is the songwriter Billy Bragg. He has participated in a much wider debate about why the English feel so unwilling to celebrate St George's Day and he has concluded that his origins and history make him a very appropriate figure to be the patron saint of England. In the issue of *Time Out* magazine for 20–27 April 2005, Bragg wrote a column about the reluctance of the English to mark the feast day of their patron saint in which he notes that, 'Sadly, St George's Day conjures up the negative image of a beer-bellied, shaven-headed lout setting his bull terrier on an asylum seeker. The great irony is that St George himself is an immigrant.' Bragg also comments that St George was given the role of patron saint of England that was previously shared by St Edward the Confessor and St Alban and makes the observation, 'That George was able to make the role his own suggests our ancestors were neither hidebound by tradition nor scared of trying something different'. For Bragg, St George has the potential to serve as an extremely appropriate and apt patron saint of an increasingly multi-ethnic England, concluding that, 'This olive-skinned stranger from the Middle East might help us slay the dragon of English xenophobia'. Bragg is pictured below the column, wearing a T-shirt which sports the flag of St George, thus suggesting that the English flag and St George himself need not only belong to the overtly nationalistic or the far-right.

Following the success of the English cricket team in regaining the Ashes in 2005, Bragg wrote a column for *The Daily Mirror* that appeared on Saturday 17 September in which he argued that the English have 'reclaimed our own flag'. For Bragg, the trend towards the adoption of the St George's flag over the Union Jack began during Euro 96 when England were drawn in the same group as the Scots. 'When the Scots came to Wembley', he wrote, 'England fans were suddenly made aware that no matter how attached to it they felt, the Union Jack wasn't actually their flag. It belonged to the British.'

As Bragg went on to discuss in the same piece, this apparent confusion of identity seems to have extended to the choice of national anthem. 'God Save the Queen', for many people, is loaded with as many uncomfortable, impe-rialistic overtones as 'Rule Britannia' and Bragg put the case for the hymn 'Jerusalem', with words by the poet William Blake, as an alternative. The idealism of the song, with its stirring words and resolve to build a utopian society in England, echoes some of the best qualities of fairness, chivalry, bravery and courage that are very often ascribed to St George.

Bibliography

The Holy Bible, New Revised Standard Version, Oxford: Oxford University Press, 1995

Barber, Richard, *The Reign of Chivalry,* Newton Abbot: David & Charles, 1980

Billings, Malcolm, *The Cross and the Crescent*, London: BBC Publications, 1987

Wallis, Sir E A Budge, *George of Lydda, The Patron Saint of England: A Study of the Cultus of St George in Ethiopia*, London: Luzac & Co, 1930

Dames, Michael, *Merlin and Wales: A Magician's Landscape*, London: Thames & Hudson, 2002

Farmer, David, *Oxford Dictionary of Saints*, Oxford: Oxford University Press, 1978

Fox, Sir David Scott, *Saint George: The Saint with Three Faces*, Windsor: Kensal Press, 1983

Gibbon, Edward, *The History of the Decline and Fall of the Roman Empire,* London: Everyman's Library, 1993

Houldcroft, Peter T, *A Pictorial Guide to Royston Cave*, Royston: Royston and District Local History Society, 1998

Hoult, Janet, *Dragons: Their History & Symbolism*, Glastonbury: Gothic Image Publications, 1987

BIBLIOGRAPHY

Hutton, Ronald, *The Rise and Fall of Merry England*, Oxford: Oxford University Press, 1994

Keen, Maurice, *English Society in the Later Middle Ages: 1348–1500*, London: Penguin, 1990

Kelly, Sean & Rogers, Rosemary, *Saints Preserve Us!*, London: Robson Books, 1993

Mann, Nicholas, *Reclaiming the Gods*, Sutton Mallet: Green Magic, 2002

Mavromataki, Maria, *Greek Mythology and Religion*, Athens: Haitalis, 1997

Michell, Jon & Rickard, Bob, *Unexplained Phenomena*, London: Rough Guides, 2000

Ormrod, W M, *The Reign of Edward III*, New Haven: Yale University Press, 1990

Riches, Samantha, *St George: Hero, Martyr and Myth*, Stroud: Sutton Publishing, 2000

Simpson, Jacqueline, *British Dragons*, London: Batsford, 1980

Smith, Godfrey, *The English Companion*, London: Pavilion, 1984

Stace, Christopher, *St George: Patron Saint of England*, London: Triangle, 2002

Voragine, Jacobus de, *The Golden Legend*, London: Penguin, 1998

Whitlock, Ralph, *Here Be Dragons*, London: George Allen & Unwin, 1983

Web Pages

www.history.uk.com
www.historytoday.uk.com
www.knyght.co.uk
www.royalsocietyofstgeorge.com
www.en.wikipedia.org/wiki/Saint_George

Index